SAVING THE SOUL OF JESUS

THE SPIRITUALITY OF JESUS... AND IT'S PRACTICE

BY JAMES A. ROBERTS

GRATITUDE TO MY TEACHERS:
JERRY JUD, MATTHEW FOX, ROBERT BLY,
ELIZABETH COGBURN, & SALLYANN

PUBLISHED BY AARDVARK GLOBAL PUBLISHING

PRINTED BY "THE PRINTING HOUSE"
STOUGHTON, WISCONSIN
PRINTED FROM EUCALYPTUS PULP,
AN ECOLOGICAL/SUSTAINABLE ALTERNATIVE TO TREES

ISBN: 978-1-4276-4433-6

FRONT COVER BY MARK JOHN HOFFMAN

PHOTOGRAPHY BY MARK BOND
(BUTTERFLY SEQUENCE BY J. ROBERTS)

"CHRIST- WINDOW" STONE LITHOGRAPH BY DAVID PANOSH

"THE DOORS" CANVAS & WOOD PAINTING BY
MARK JOHN HOFFMAN

"THE RIVER OF LIFE" WINDOW IS AT EMMANUEL
LUTHERAN CHURCH. ROCKFORD, ILL.

HEART-FELT THANKS TO THESE ARTISTS AND TO THE PEOPLE

OF EMMANUEL LUTHERAN CHURCH IN ROCKFORD, ILL.

WHO SO BRAVELY ENTERED THE SPIRITUALITY OF JESUS.

TABLE OF CONTENTS

THE VISION: WHY I HAD
TO WRITE THIS...

"It is the fall of 1979. I get into the church's pulpit after being a pastor for 10 years and I KNOW NOW THAT I AM LOST.

I am a good pastor, but I have no real connection to God.

My life is a lie. Stumbling through words, I cautiously dare to own up to this in the sermon and add that I want to find my way through this dark forest.

After the service an older woman takes my hand and puts her other hand over mine as if to hold me...

She says, "We'll pray for you". She must have...

In that tender, fractured moment something gestated in me. And I went on a journey to find myself and rediscover Jesus, who had captivated me in my youth.

This is our story. Let's begin with Jesus."

JESUS IS ALWAYS SEEN THROUGH A PAIR OF LENSES.
   THERE ARE DOCTRINAL LENSES...
   THE TRINITY: JESUS AS TRUE GOD, TRUE MAN;
   THE SINLESSNESS OF JESUS; THE ONLY SON OF GOD;
   THE SPOTLESS SACRIFICE FOR SIN; ... ETC.

I FOUND IT DIFFICULT, IF NOT IMPOSSIBLE,
   TO MAKE A CONNECTION WITH JESUS
         THROUGH THESE LENSES.
   **IT WAS WHEN I EXPERIENCED THE SPIRITUAL JOURNEY
         FOR A LONG TIME,**
   THAT I **BEGAN TO CONNECT**
   WITH THE JOURNEY OF JESUS AND
   SEE PARALLELS TO MY OWN EXPERIENCE.

FOR EXAMPLE:

   WHEN I WAS IN THE MOUNTAINS OF NEW MEXICO ALONE,
   FASTING & PRAYING & WRESTLING WITH MYSELF & GOD
         FOR 4 DAYS,
   I GOT A GLIMPSE OF WHAT JESUS WAS DOING IN THE
         DESERT FOR 40 DAYS.
   I UNDERSTOOD IN A VISCERAL WAY AND
         HAD A NEW FEELING
         FOR HIS INTENSITY, LONGING, AND COURAGE.
   HE BECAME REAL AND ACCESSIBLE TO ME.
   WE BEGAN A BOND OF FRIENDSHIP.
   HE BECAME SOMEONE I COULD FOLLOW.

WHEN JESUS TRAVELED TO BE WITH JOHN
    AT THE JORDAN RIVER,
I DIDN'T GET IT UNTIL I WAS SO DESPERATE **_MYSELF_**
    FOR AN AUTHENTIC SPIRIT-PERSON.
I WAS WILLING TO GO **_ANYWHERE_** TO FIND A TRUE MENTOR,
    SOMEONE I COULD REALLY LEARN FROM.

AND WHEN I DID, I SAW IT EVOLVE
    INTO SOMETHING "MUTUAL".
I SAW THIS ALSO HAPPEN WITH JESUS AND JOHN.
I UNDERSTOOD.
I LIKED THAT JESUS REALLY NEEDED THAT
    AND WENT AFTER IT.
JESUS BECAME MORE REAL & ACCESSIBLE.

THEN AT JESUS' BAPTISM,
HE HAS A PROFOUND EXPERIENCE
    OF THE DIVINE BELOVED.
THAT BECAME REAL & ACCESSIBLE _ONLY_
WHEN MY OWN LONGING FOR GOD CRACKED ME OPEN,
AND ALL THAT MATTERED WAS THE DIVINE EMBRACE.
AND I FELL IN LOVE WITH THE BELOVED.

MY STUDY & MEDITATION ON JESUS' LIFE HAS CONTINUALLY
    UNVEILED A REAL HUMAN BEING
    WHO IS SO AMAZING TO ME
    THAT HIS LIFE CONTINUES TO LIVE ON IN ME.
    AND I GET SOME OF HIS SPIRIT & COURAGE &
    COMPASSION & LONGING MYSTERIOUSLY THROUGH
    OUR REAL & ACCESSIBLE CONNECTION.

JESUS HAS BECOME MENTOR, BROTHER, SOUL-FRIEND...

I CAN'T DESCRIBE THIS WELL IN THEOLOGY,
    DOCTRINE,
    OR CREED.
I'LL LEAVE THAT TO OTHERS.
I HAVE TROUBLE EVEN USING WORDS,
BUT HERE IS MY SINCERE ATTEMPT TO DESCRIBE
THE JOURNEY OF JESUS
AS IT HAS BECOME REAL
    & ACCESSIBLE
    & LUMINOUS FOR ME.

JESUS IS NOT JUST FOR CHRISTIANS.
    JESUS IS A GIFT TO HUMANITY.
    SOMETIMES OTHERS OUTSIDE OF CHRISTIANITY
    CAN HELP US SEE JESUS IN FRESH WAYS.

THICH NHAT HANH IS A VIETNAMESE BUDDHIST
   WHO WRITES ABOUT JESUS.   [1]
   HE IS INSPIRED, MOVED, TAUGHT BY JESUS.
   AND YOU CAN SEE IT IN THICH'S LIFE: HIS WAY
    OF INTEGRITY, PEACE, AND COMPASSION.

IT'S TIME FOR ALL THE WORLD TO RECEIVE
   THIS GIFT OF GOD:
   NOT TO JOIN A CHURCH,
   OR EVEN BECOME CHRISTIAN,
   BUT TO MAKE A CONNECTION WITH THIS LIFE,
   WHETHER CHRISTIAN OR BUDDHIST,
   JEW OR MUSLIM,
   HINDU OR PAGAN...

MAYBE WE CAN ALL LEARN COMPASSION
   & JUSTICE
   & FORGIVENESS

   AND LEARN HOW TO **LIVE WITH EACH OTHER**

   AND WITH THE **STRANGER** AMONG US,

   WHO IS OFTEN ACTUALLY
      "OUR OWN SELVES".

HOW URGENT IS OUR TIME....

PRELUDE

JESUS IS TOO IMPORTANT TO BE CONFINED TO RELIGION. JESUS HAS
BEEN WRAPPED IN DOCTRINAL GRAVE CLOTHES
   AND BURIED UNDER 2000 YEARS OF CONTROVERSY,
   COUNCILS, SCHISMS, EVEN WARS...
HE HAS BEEN BOUGHT, SOLD, BARTERED, AND BETRAYED.
JESUS HAS BEEN SILENT THROUGH THIS.....

   EXCEPT FOR **VISITATIONS** IN OUR NIGHTLY DREAMS,
   FILLING OUR MINDS WITH SEARING IMAGES OF COMPASSION
   HAUNTING US WITH HIS HUNGER FOR THE BELOVED
   FLARING FORTH HIS SPIRIT INTO SOMEONE'S LUMINOUS LIFE

AND JESUS HAS DISTURBED MY SLEEP,
   ETCHED HIS STORIES INTO MY MIND, AND FLOODED ME
   WITH LONGING FOR A DEEPER LIVING.
I HAVE FALLEN IN LOVE WITH THIS ONE
   AND I AM NOT THE SAME FOR IT.

AND SO YOU SEE THAT I HAD TO WRITE THIS.
   THIS IS ABOUT THE LAST 44 YEARS THAT
   WE HAVE BEEN ON THIS JOURNEY TOGETHER.
   ALONG THE WAY I HAVE DISCOVERED
   MORE OF WHO THIS JESUS IS AND SURPRISINGLY,
   THAT BEGAN TO REVEAL THE MYSTERY OF WHO I AM.

THE UNVEILINGS ARE ENTWINED, OF COURSE. LET'S BEGIN....

THE FLOWERING OF THE HUMAN

THE "JESUS" I HAVE COME TO KNOW HAS EXPANDED THE
   VISION OF WHAT IT COULD BE TO BE "HUMAN".
IF THE "HUMAN" WAS A BUD,
   JESUS OPENED TO THE SUN
      AND "FLOWERED".
   THIS OPENING AND STRETCHING WAS
      LUMINOUS AND STUNNING.
    IT INSPIRED AND CHALLENGED "HUMANS"
      TO SEE WHAT WE COULD BE.

WE COULDN'T PRETEND WE DIDN'T SEE THIS!
   (COULD WE?)

WHAT ABOUT....

PRESENCE

HOW AMAZINGLY PRESENT JESUS WAS!
   AS SIMPLE A THING AS BEING FULLY PRESENT
      TO THE BEAUTY OF THE CREATION,
   THE EXPERIENCE OF THIS RICH MOMENT,
   THE "OH SO HUMAN" FACE BEFORE YOU ...
   THAT IS HEALING AND EMPOWERING.
   WHAT IS THE STILLNESS OF SOUL THAT
      ALLOWS JESUS TO BE SO
      UNDISTRACTED AND ROOTED?

RADICAL INTIMACY WITH THE DIVINE

JESUS GOES INTO THE DIVINE
     AS ONE DIVES INTO A RIVER.
MEISTER ECKHART DESCRIBES GOD
     AS A GREAT UNDERGROUND RIVER. [2]
IT'S GREAT TO WATCH A RIVER FLOW,
     BUT TO GO INTO THE RIVER IS SOMETHING ELSE.
JESUS HAD A PROFOUND IMMERSION
     IN THE DIVINE BELOVED.
WHEN RELIGIOUS PEOPLE STAY DRY,
     THEN WE ARE LEFT WITH BELIEF SYSTEMS,
     MUCH WRITING AND TALK,
     AND MANY VIEWS FROM THE BRIDGE.
HOW DO WE GO INTO THIS SACRED RIVER OF GOD?

COMPASSION & CREATIVE ENGAGEMENT

JESUS STRETCHED INSIDE THE SOUL
     AND STRETCHED OUTSIDE AS WELL.
HE CHALLENGED THE EMPTINESS OF THE CULTURE,
     THE STERILITY OF RELIGION,
     AND THE OPPRESSION OF THE
     "ANAWIM" (HEBREW:THE POWERLESS & POOR ONES).
HE CREATED A SMALL COMMUNITY TO BEGIN
     TO LIVE AN ALTERNATIVE LIFESTYLE, A BAND OF
     "ENGAGED MYSTICS", "PROPHETIC CONTEMPLATIVES"...

THERE WAS AN ANCIENT TRADITION OF THIS
     DIVING INTO THE DIVINE PRESENCE
     <u>COMBINED</u> WITH COMPASSIONATE &
     PROPHETIC ENGAGEMENT WITH ONE'S CULTURE,
     BUT IT WAS RARE AND IN THE CASE OF THE
      HEBREW PROPHETS, PERSONALLY DANGEROUS.

WHEN RELIGION GETS CAUGHT UP IN ITSELF,
"PRESENCE" COLLAPSES TO "SHOWING UP"
OR SERVING ON COMMITTEES
"INTIMACY WITH DIVINE" BECOMES
BELIEF SYSTEMS
AND PERFORMED PRAYERS
"COMPASSION / ENGAGEMENT" BECOMES
CONTRIBUTIONS TO CHARITIES

THERE IS NOTHING WRONG WITH COMMITTEES,
BELIEF SYSTEMS, OR CONTRIBUTIONS....

BUT JESUS DID NOT GIVE HIMSELF SO THOROUGHLY,
OR LIVE SO DEEPLY *ONLY FOR THIS*.

*WE WANT THE HEART AND SOUL OF JESUS NOW,
OR LET US JUST GO HUNGRY AWAY.*

THERE HAVE BEEN ENOUGH BELIEF SYSTEMS ABOUT JESUS.
THERE ARE ENOUGH CONFESSIONS,
CREEDS AND SALVITIC FORMULAS.
THERE ARE ENOUGH BUILDINGS AND COMMITTEES
AND GOLD CROSSES.

IT'S TIME FOR THE SPIRITUALITY OF JESUS. AND

IT'S TIME FOR THE PRACTICE OF JESUS' SPIRITUALITY!

COME, EVERYONE WHO LONGS TO KNOW WHAT IT IS
TO BE TRULY AN EMBODIED, INSPIRITED HUMAN.

THIS IS NOT ABOUT RELIGION ANYMORE,

THIS IS ABOUT THE **SANCTITY OF LIFE** ON THIS PLANET,

AND THE **FLOWERING OF THE HUMAN!**

THE TREASURE IN THE FIELD

JESUS SAID, *"THE KINGDOM OF HEAVEN IS LIKE*
TREASURE HIDDEN IN A FIELD WHICH SOMEONE HAS FOUND;
HE HIDES IT AGAIN, GOES OFF IN HIS JOY,
SELLS EVERYTHING HE OWNS
AND BUYS THE FIELD."   MATTHEW 13:44

YOU TRIP OVER THIS THING ON YOUR WAY SOMEWHERE ELSE!
YOU GO ON A RETREAT... YOU FALL IN LOVE... YOU ARE MOVED BY A
LUMINOUS DREAM... YOU TOUCH THE NOUMENOUS... YOU ARE
OVERWHELMED WITH LONGING...YOU AWAKEN...

"THAT'S GOOD", JESUS MIGHT SAY...
    "NOW YOU KNOW THAT THERE IS SOMETHING MORE,
     BUT ITS BEEN HIDDEN FROM YOUR SIGHT,
     IGNORED BY YOUR CONSCIOUSNESS.
    HOWEVER, IT IS A **REAL TREASURE**,

    BUT NOT THE KIND THAT OTHER PEOPLE MAY GET
    EXCITED ABOUT... LIKE YOUR SPOUSE, OR YOUR FRIENDS
    OR FAMILY... OR FATHER.
    AND SO **YOU GO ON** WITH YOUR NORMAL LIFE".

BUT YOU WILL ALSO BE TORMENTED BECAUSE YOU HAVE
    SEEN IT AND YOU HAVE GONE ON, AND YOU WILL FIND A
    HAUNTING FAILURE IN EVERYTHING YOU DO
    WHILE YOU RUN FROM IT.

JESUS MIGHT SAY, "YOU HAVE FOUND THIS TREASURE,
    THE GREAT TREASURE OF THE SOUL.
    PEOPLE HAVE SEARCHED FOR DECADES TO FIND THIS.
    THIS IS THE HOLY GRAIL, THE PEARL OF GREAT PRICE AND
    SO YOU NEED TO OWN THIS!
    MAKE IT YOUR OWN!
    SET YOUR HEART ON IT,
    SELL EVERYTHING YOU HAVE...
    TO BUY THIS FIELD!...
    OWN THIS TREASURE!
    BELONG TO THE DESTINY OF THAT TREASURE!

BUYING THAT FIELD IS THE INVESTMENT OF
    YOUR ENERGY & PASSION IN THIS TREASURE.

PRACTICING THE SPIRITUALITY OF JESUS IS THE INVESTMENT.

PRACTICING THE SPIRITUALITY OF JESUS IS BUYING THE FIELD.

"It is 1998 and I am talking to a group of pastors about a retreat we're leading on "Jonah & our call from God". I say it won't be a seminar, but will focus on our connection to God and explore what our own "call" really is. I was excited about this, but there is silence.........
As I left, one man, a pastor for 25 years, courageously said, "It's not that we aren't interested. It's just that we're scared. I know now what I need. I need a spirituality." Then he leaned in to whisper,......
"But I don't even know what that is."

WELL, WHAT IS IT? LET'S BEGIN WITH **JESUS' SPIRITUALITY**.

THE FIRST CENTURY IN THE MIDDLE EAST
    WAS A TIME OF SIMMERING CHAOS.
      SOCIAL CLASS, WEALTH & POVERTY DIVIDED PEOPLE
        WHO WERE ALL SUBJUGATED BY THE
        PAGAN EMPIRE OF ROME.
      MANY JEWS WERE DRAWN INTO VIOLENCE
        & REVOLUTION BY THE OPPRESSION.
INTO THIS SHATTERED CULTURE CAME PROPHETS
    LIKE JOHN THE BAPTIST CALLING PEOPLE
    BACK TO THEIR RELIGIOUS ROOTS.
AND THEN CAME JESUS WITH A REVOLUTION FAR DEEPER
    AND MORE EXTENSIVE THAN ANY ZEALOT.
THIS IS HIS MESSAGE AND HIS REVOLUTION,
    STILL AS RADICAL & FAR-REACHING... EVEN MORE TIMELY.

A) THE MESSAGE OF JESUS: MARK 1:15

JESUS CAME TO JOHN TO BE INITIATED
    INTO THIS NEW SPIRIT MOVEMENT
    OUT IN THE DESERT AROUND THE JORDAN RIVER.
JOHN INVITES JESUS INTO THE RIVER FOR A
    CLEANSING CEREMONY & NEW BEGINNING.
    JESUS HAS A POWERFUL IMMERSION INTO GOD.
      WORDS OF GRACE ENVELOP HIM.
      HE COMES OUT OF THE RIVER,
        BUT THE RIVER REMAINS WITHIN.

IT SAYS THAT VERY SPIRIT DROVE HIM INTO SOLITUDE &
    MEDITATION & FASTING FOR 40 DAYS IN THE DESERT
    (YOU CAN LIVE 45 DAYS WITHOUT FOOD).
    THERE HE WRESTLES WITH HIMSELF & GOD

COMING OUT WITH A CALL & A MESSAGE.
("ISRAEL" MEANS "THOSE WHO WRESTLE WITH GOD")
JESUS' MESSAGE IS DIRECT AND SUCCINCT IN MARK 1:15:

"THE TIME IS FULFILLED. THE KINGDOM OF GOD HAS COME NEAR; REPENT AND BELIEVE IN THE GOOD NEWS"

LET'S LOOK AT **EACH** OF THE FOUR PARTS:

"THE TIME IS FULFILLED".

THERE ARE 2 GREEK WORDS FOR TIME.
  "**CHRONOS**" IS REGULAR TIME. YOUR WATCH KEEPS THAT.
  IT'S A PREDICTABLE STRUCTURE FOR LIVING.
THE OTHER IS "**KAIROS**", WHICH IS AN "OUT OF TIME" TIME,
  AN OPPORTUNE, CRACK BETWEEN THE WORLDS,
  BREAKING-IN, BREAKING-OPEN, DECISIVE TIME.
  THIS IS A TIME TO "WAKE-UP!"
  WHAT YOU'VE BEEN WAITING FOR,
  OR GAVE UP LOOKING FOR, IS **HERE**!
WE HAVE TO BREAK OUT OF OUR CAPTIVITY TO "CHRONOS"
  AND *FALL* INTO "KAIROS", OR WE WILL MISS THIS.

"THE KINGDOM OF GOD HAS COME NEAR".

JESUS TALKED ABOUT THIS REIGN OF GOD
  MORE THAN **ANYTHING** ELSE.
  AS TODAY, IT WAS OFTEN THOUGHT OF AS SOMETHING
  THAT EXISTED IN THE "NEXT" WORLD AND SO WOULD
  BREAK IN AT THE CATACLYSMIC END OF THIS WORLD
  OR SOMEHOW AFTER ONE DIED.

BUT JESUS SAW IT BREAKING IN **NOW & EVEN HERE**!

THIS WAS THE URGENCY & THE EXCITEMENT AROUND JESUS. THE PHARISEES (A "BACK TO THE BIBLE" REFORM MOVEMENT
                              IN JUDIASM) DEMANDED,

*"WHEN WILL THE REIGN OF GOD COME?" JESUS SAID,
"THE REIGN OF GOD COMES NOT WITH OBSERVATION; NEITHER SHALL THEY SAY, 'LO HERE! OR LO THERE!
FOR BEHOLD, THE REIGN OF GOD
    IS AMONG (OR WITHIN) YOU".* LUKE 17:20

"WHEN WILL THE REPOSE OF THE DEAD COME ABOUT
    AND WHEN WILL THE NEW WORLD COME?"
JESUS SAID, "WHAT YOU ARE WAITING FOR
    HAS ALREADY COME, BUT YOU DO NOT REALIZE IT."
        GOSPEL OF THOMAS 51   [3]

THIS IS AN OLD BIBLICAL THEME. GOD IS PRESENT,
    BUT WE HAVE LOST THE ABILITY TO PERCEIVE.

JACOB, AFTER HIS SACRED DREAM SAYS,

"GOD WAS SURELY IN THIS PLACE,
    AND I DIDN'T KNOW IT...
    HOW AWE INSPIRING THIS PLACE IS!
    THIS IS NOTHING LESS THAN THE ABODE OF GOD,
    AND THIS IS THE GATE OF HEAVEN!" GENESIS 28:17F.

EVEN WHEN THE SPIRIT COMES DOWN AT PENTECOST,
    YOU MAY HEAR THE SINGING, BUT MISS THE PRESENCE.
THIS IS A GREAT ENERGY OF GOD BREAKING IN
    TO HEAL THE WORLD, BEGINNING **INSIDE** YOU.
    DO YOU FEEL SOMETHING STIRRING INSIDE?
    DO YOU HEAR YOUR NAME BEING CALLED?
    OR DO YOU PERCEIVE SOMETHING
        BREAKING IN **AROUND** YOU?
    ARE YOU AWAKENING TO THE BEAUTY OF GOD
            EVERYWHERE AROUND YOU?
    OR IS IT THE PRESENCE OF A **GREAT LOVE**?
    DO YOU FEEL YOURSELF WITHIN THE "**ABODE OF GOD**"?

THIS IS A CALL TO SEE WITH NEW EYES
    AND FEEL WITH A HEART OF FLESH, NOT STONE.

NOTE THAT THIS IS **NOT** THE REIGN OF ISRAEL,
    OR OF THE U.S.A.,
    OR OF CHRISTIANITY;
    BUT OF GOD.
THIS IS THE ONE WHO HOLDS **ALL** THE PEOPLE
    AND THE **WHOLE** CREATION.
LET NO ONE DARE FEIGN CONTROL OF THE REIGN OF GOD.

"REPENT"
THE GREEK WORD "METANOIA" IS
    OFTEN TRANSLATED AS "REPENT".
    REPENTANCE HAD MEANT "FEELING SORRY"

FOR WHAT YOU HAD DONE,
A KIND OF MOURNING AND CONFESSION,
IN THE HOPE OF BEING FORGIVEN.
ACTUALLY, "**METANOIA**" MEANS A
RADICAL TRANSFORMATION AKIN TO
THE WORD "**METAMORPHOSIS**".
NOTE IN THE PHOTOS, THE TRANSFORMATION OF AN EGG
INTO A CATERPILLAR, THEN INTO A CHRYSALIS,
AND THEN INTO A BUTTERFLY.
NOW THAT'S "METANOIA"!
THE EGG DOESN'T JUST MOURN BEING AN EGG,
OR "REPENT" OF ITS LIMITATIONS AS AN EGG.
IT CRACKS OPEN,
AND BEGINS ITS NEW LIFE AS A CATERPILLAR.

IN A METAPHOR JESUS TALKS ABOUT THE NECESSITY
OF A SINGLE GRAIN OF WHEAT (SMALL SELF)
TO GO INTO THE DARK GROUND
AND DIE (BREAK APART, LOSE ITSELF)
IN ORDER FOR THE ROOT, SHOOT, PLANT, GRAINS, AND
BREAD (GREATER SELF) TO BE MANIFEST. (JOHN 12:24)

JESUS IS TALKING ABOUT ENTERING A PROCESS
WHERE WE LEAVE OUR FORMER SELVES,
GET CAUGHT UP IN THE MYSTERY OF THE BELOVED,
AND DISCOVER THAT WE WEREN'T WHO WE THOUGHT
WE WERE WHEN WE BEGAN THIS.
IN FACT,

WE ARE WHO THE BELOVED THOUGHT WE WERE.

THAT IS WHAT JESUS IS TALKING ABOUT!
THE SPIRIT IS MOVING THROUGH THIS PLACE.
NOW, WHAT ARE WE TO DO?.....   **METAMORPHOSE!!!!**
BEGIN THE SHIFT FROM JUDGMENT TO FORGIVENESS,
FROM A HUMAN-EYED VIEW TO A GOD'S-EYE VIEW,
FROM ARROGANCE TO COMPASSION,
FROM SOCIAL CLASS TO COMMUNITY,
FROM FEAR TO CREATIVITY,
FROM EGO CENTER TO SOUL CENTER.
WE NEED A NEW WINESKIN FOR THIS NEW WINE!

MOST OF JESUS' TEACHING IS ALL ABOUT THIS
METAMORPHOSIS FROM THE "OLD HUMAN"
TO THE "NEW HUMAN". THIS IS AN EVOLUTION.
IT IS CLEAR THAT I CAN'T GO ON IN
THE SAME OLD "CHRONOS" WAY.

WE ONLY JUST GET OLDER THAT WAY
    AND WE KNOW WHAT THAT IS LIKE.

THE ONLY RIGHT RESPONSE TO "KAIROS" IS "METAMORPHOSIS!

MY WIFE, SALLYANN, RAISES MONARCH BUTTERFLIES.
    I AM ALWAYS MOVED AT HOW THE CATERPILLAR EATS &
    EATS AND GETS BIGGER & BIGGER UNTIL "KAIROS".
    SOMETHING CALLS TO IT OF IT'S DESTINY, IT'S EVOLUTION.
THEN IT STOPS EATING, FINDS A HIGH PLACE TO
    ATTACH ITSELF, AND HANGS UPSIDE DOWN,
    CURLING INTO A "J".
    IT DOESN'T WHINE OR PROCRASTINATE.
    THEN IT SPLITS OPEN AND TRANSFORMS MAGICALLY
    INTO A CHRYSALIS: A GREEN ABODE WITH BEAUTIFUL GOLD
    GLITTER ON IT.
    THEN IT SILENTLY OFFERS ITSELF TO ITS DESTINY TO ADORN
    THE WORLD WITH ITS VULNERABLE BEAUTY, ITS MAGICAL FLIGHT,
    AND IT'S DRAMATIC ENCOURAGEMENT TO ALL.

A BUTTERFLY'S METAMORPHOSIS

NOTE THE PICTURES OF THE JOURNEY OF A MONARCH.
MEDITATE ON THESE PICTURES...

HOW DO THEY SPEAK TO YOU OF ***YOUR OWN METAMORPHOSIS***?

WITH WHAT PICTURE DO YOU MOST *IDENTIFY*
    NOW IN YOUR LIFE?

NOTICE HOW SOME STAGES ARE VERY SMALL (EGG)
    AND INTERIOR.
OTHERS ARE ACTIVE AND INTENSE
        (CATERPILLARS EAT & GROW CONTINUALLY).
 STILL OTHERS APPEAR LIKE A DEATH
        (THE LONG STILLNESS OF THE CHRYSALIS FOR WEEKS).
 ANOTHER IS SURPRISING AND STUNNING
        (EMERGENCE OF THE BUTTERFLY).

EACH STAGE IS UNIQUE AND SURPRISINGLY DISTINCT.

WHAT DOES IT MEAN NOW TO
    HEAR JESUS SAY TO YOU:

    "METAMORPHOSE!"?

"BELIEVE IN THE GOOD NEWS,

"TRUST" IS A BETTER WORD HERE.
>   THIS IS A CALL TO TRUST.
>   HAVE FAITH IN THE DIVINE AND THE SPIRIT-MOVEMENT
>   WHICH CAN SO EASILY GO UNRECOGNIZED.
>   JESUS SAID THAT IF WE HAD TRUST THE SIZE OF
>   A TINY SEED, LIFE WOULD TRANSFORM AROUND US.

NICODEMUS (JOHN 3) CAME TO JESUS WITH THE
>   BELIEF SYSTEM OF A RESPECTED RELIGIOUS LEADER,
>   BUT WITHOUT **TRUST** IN GOD'S POWER OR
>   PRESENCE IN HIS OWN LIFE.
>   SO HE COULD **SEE NO NEW BEGINNING,**
>   **NO METANOIA, NO DIVINE ENERGY,**
>   **NO NEW BIRTH** FOR HIM.
>   HE WAS JUST AN OLD, TIRED MAN.

SO FOR ALL OF US WHO HAVE MISSED GOD'S PRESENCE,
>   NOT TASTED THE DIVINE FIRE,
>   ARE WEARY OF OUR BROKEN CULTURE,
>   FEEL STUCK IN AN OLD WINESKIN AND LIFESTYLE,
>   OR ARE HOPELESSLY ADDICTED TO A LITTLE EGO-LIFE....
>   **THIS** IS A REFRESHING CHANCE FOR A NEW BEGINNING.
>   THIS COMES AS HOPE AND VERY **GOOD NEWS** INDEED.

IF THE 1ST RESPONSE IS TRANSFORMATION,

>   THEN THE 2ND IS TRUST...
>   OR IS IT THE OTHER WAY AROUND?

SO WE COULD PARAPHRASE JESUS' MESSAGE
>   FROM MARK 1:15 AS:

> *"WAKE UP!*
> *SEIZE THIS MOMENT FOR A NEW BEGINNING.*
> *GOD'S SPIRIT IS MOVING AROUND YOU*
>   *AND INSIDE YOU.*
>   *(CAN YOU PERCEIVE THIS?)*
> *BE TRANSFORMED AND*
>   *RADICALLY TRUST*
>   *IN THIS GREAT NEWS!"*

REFLECTIONS ON THE REIGN OF GOD

IT IS A PARTLY CLOUDY AUGUST DAY
   IN MY NEIGHBORHOOD OF ROCKFORD, ILLINOIS.
   A BREEZE IS MOVING THE LEAVES.
   A MAN WALKS HIS DOG.
   CHILDREN ARE PLAYING.
   HOW VERY ORDINARY...

WHAT WE ARE TALKING ABOUT HERE
   IS NOT <u>ANOTHER REALITY</u>,

BUT A <u>WAY OF SEEING</u>...

   WHERE *WE SEE WHAT IS AROUND US.*
   AND IT IS NO LONGER ORDINARY REALITY,
   BUT REALITY STRIPPED NAKED OF ITS ORDINARINESS,
   TO REVEAL ITS INTRINSIC BEAUTY AND RADIANCE...
      THE SHIMMERING FIELD AROUND EVERYTHING...
      FIELDS OF ENERGY PULSE
      AND DANCE WITH COLOR & LIGHT,
      AND THERE IS NO ORDINARY CHILD.

AND A <u>WAY OF EXPERIENCING</u>...

   WHERE THE SUN'S PHOTON SHOWER
     IS SOAKED INTO THE SKIN
     IN AN OUTRAGEOUS EFFUSION OF GRACE.
     (THE SUN GIVES AWAY TONS OF ITSELF EACH SECOND)
   AND THE MOVING CLOUD SHAPES ARE
     A CONSTANTLY CHANGING
     GALLERY OF ART.
   AND THE WIND'S CARESS
     IS THE SPIRIT'S REFRESHING EMBRACE.

AND A <u>WAY OF RELATING</u>...

   THE STRANGER WALKING HIS DOG
     IS STRANGELY RELATED.
     HIS LONELINESS IS ABSORBED,
     AND HIS LONGING TO BE CONNECTED
     DRAWS ME TO HIM.
     WHAT MOVES IN HIM,
       MOVES IN ME
     AND HIS DOG SEES MY PAIN.

IS THE REIGN OF GOD SIMPLY
    SEEING,
    EXPERIENCING,
    RELATING
      TO WHAT WE HAVE BECOME
      BLIND TO,
      NUMB TOWARD, AND
      DISCONNECTED FROM?

WHAT IF IT IS SIMPLY
    ALL ..... AROUND...... US?

AND WE ONLY HAVE TO
    OPEN OURSELVES TO IT?

THE GOOD NEWS IS THAT
    IT IS RIGHT HERE!

AND IT IS *"KAIROS"*
    WHEN *WE OPEN OUR EYES,*
    OUR HEART,
    AND OUR WORLD.

IS THIS WHAT JESUS MEANT
    WHEN HE SAID
    "THE REIGN OF GOD IS AT HAND...
      AMONG YOU...
      WITHIN YOU?"

THAT IT'S ALL HERE......................
    WAITING FOR ME TO ARRIVE.

WE **TRAVEL** TO ESCAPE THE ORDINARY & ROUTINE...

BUT WHAT IF THE WAY
TO ESCAPE THE ORDINARY & ROUTINE
   IS.....   **THE OPENING OF EYES**

    THE ENTERING INTO THE PRESENT

    THE CONNECTING WITH WHAT IS?

AND WE CAN DO THAT..
    ANYWHERE...
      EVEN RIGHT HERE...
       EVEN NOW.

ANOTHER REFLECTION
ON THE REIGN OF GOD...

THE *REIGN OF GOD* WAS NOT
THE REIGN OF JUDIASM,
or CHRISTIANITY, OR RELIGION.

BUT IT WAS JESUS' CONTINUAL REFRAIN
To *E X P A N D* OUR HEART & MIND
BEYOND OUR LITTLE *EGOS*

BEYOND OUR *PERSONAL FAMILY*

BEYOND OUR LITTLE *CONGREGATION & RELIGION*

BEYOND OUR FOCUS ONLY ON "*HUMANS*"

To THE

WHOLE CREATION...

THE ENTIRE MAGNIFICENT UNIVERSE OF GOD

B) THE INWARD JOURNEY OF JESUS

"It is 1976 and I'm in a bible study with pastors. The text, which comes up annually, is the baptism of Jesus in the Jordan River. I say that this is really important.
Others look at me and the leader says,
'What's the big deal about the baptism of Jesus?'
I have no answer. I don't understand what is going on
in Jesus.   I fall silent..."

JESUS HAS AN HUGE INWARD JOURNEY.
   AND WE HAVE SOME RECORD OF IT'S RICHNESS,
   EVEN THOUGH JESUS' FOLLOWERS
         SEEM TO BE BAFFLED BY IT.
WE HAVE JESUS IN THE RIVER... IN THE DESERT...
   ACROSS THE LAKE...
   IN EARLY MORNING PRAYER TIMES...
   IN AN ALL NIGHT VIGIL...
   IN THE GARDEN OF GETHSEMANE PRAYING...
   IN THE TRANSFIGURATION MEDITATION
         ON THE MOUNTAIN... ETC.
THIS IS ONLY INDICATIVE OF THE DEVOTION
   TO THE INNER LIFE THAT JESUS HAD.
   WE CAN'T GO FAR WITH JESUS WITHOUT ENTERING
         SOME KIND OF INWARD JOURNEY.
WE ALSO KNOW ONLY TOO WELL
   HOW IT IS POSSIBLE TO HAVE AN
   ENGAGED OUTWARD JOURNEY,
      AND BE VERY RELIGIOUS AT THAT,
   AND LOSE THE INWARD JOURNEY ALONG THE WAY.
   I DID IT. I WAS REALLY GOOD AT IT.
   I KNOW <u>ALL</u> ABOUT THAT.

TO BEGIN TO GRASP THE VASTNESS OF JESUS' INWARD
   JOURNEY, LET'S LOOK AT IT IN TWO PARTS:
   "IMMERSING IN THE WILD & TENDER DIVINE"
   AND **"EMBRACING THE SHADOW"**.

<u>"IMMERSING IN THE WILD & TENDER DIVINE"</u>

THIS "IMMERSION" PICKS UP
   WHERE THE **"DIVINE IMAGE"** WITHIN HIM
   WAS LEADING HIM... RIGHT INTO THE DIVINE **PRESENCE**.
OTHERS BEFORE HIM HAD GONE DEEPLY INTO THE "ONE",
   THE GREAT "I AM".

BUT THERE IS SOMETHING SO COMPELLING ABOUT
JESUS' EXPERIENCE THAT MAKES **YOU** WANT TO GO THERE TOO.
MARK 1:12 STATES:
" *THE SPIRIT DROVE HIM INTO THE DESERT TO BE*
    CHALLENGED BY THE ADVERSARY
    (MEANING OF "SATANA" IN GREEK), AND HE WAS
    WITH THE WILD ANIMALS & ANGELS"

THIS CAPTURES HIS SPIRITUALITY.
    THE **WILD ANIMALS** HAD A FIERCENESS, PASSION,
    INDEPENDENCE, AND WILDNESS
    THAT WAS **IMPLANTED IN THE ANIMALS** BY THE DIVINE
    AND WAS **TRANSPLANTED INTO JESUS.**

SO WHEN HE CAME OUT OF THE DESERT,
    JESUS HAD THAT PASSION & WILDNESS IN HIM.
    AND HE WOULD NEED EVERY BIT OF THAT.
    HE COULDN'T BE TAMED, DOMESTICATED AFTER THAT.
    IT WAS A SACRED WILDNESS, AN HOLY FIRE.

AND THE **ANGELS** EMBODY THE TENDERNESS OF GOD WHICH BREAKS
OPEN THE HEART AS JESUS HEARS GOD CRY OUT:
                "BELOVED, MY BELOVED"!
        JESUS CRIES BACK: *"MY BELOVED"!*
IT IS A LOVE STORY.
WE TOO DESIRE TO BE IMMERSED IN THIS
        "WILD & TENDER ONE".
WE DARE TO TRUST THIS IS ***FOR US***, TOO.

WE CRY OUT, *"BELOVED. WE COME TO YOU...*
    WE WANT LIKE JESUS TO BE "IMMERSED IN YOU"!
SOME OF US HAVE BEEN LONGING ALL OUR LIVES FOR THIS...

"EMBRACING THE SHADOW"

THE "SHADOW" INCLUDES THOSE PARTS OF US
    THAT ARE HARD TO SEE, AT LEAST BY OURSELVES.
    I WILL FOCUS ON THREE THINGS THAT ARE PART OF US,
    BUT DIFFICULT TO SEE, EVEN DISOWNED BY US.
    THEY ARE THE "**EGO-CENTRIC EGO**",
            OUR "**WOUNDS**",
            AND THE "**DIVINE IMAGE**".

SHADOW 101 : "THE EGO-CENTRIC EGO"

THE EGO IS NECESSARY FOR US TO DEVELOP AS WE GROW UP.
WE NEED A STRONG SENSE OF OURSELVES TO DO
    WHAT WE NEED TO DO IN THE WORLD,
    ESP. IN THE FACE OF OPPOSITION OR LITTLE SUPPORT.
ONCE THAT IDENTITY IS ESTABLISHED,
    THE ISSUE BECOMES FINDING SOMETHING LARGER
    THAN ONE'S EGO.
WITHOUT THAT WE ARE LEFT CAUGHT
    IN THE EGO-CENTRIC EGO ALONE,
    AN EGO-ONLY WORLD OF SELF-ABSORPTION & STRUGGLE.
IN FACT,
    OUR CULTURE CAN EVEN PROMOTE THIS "NARCISSISM".

FRITZ KUNKLE LOOKS AT FOUR DIFFERENT KINDS
    OF EGO-CENTRISM.   [4]

THOSE FROM A **HARSH** ENVIRONMENT TAKE TWO FORMS:
    A) **NERO** : SEEKS TO CONTROL/ DOMINATE OTHERS
                (EXTROVERTED FORM)
    B) **TURTLE** : SEEKS TO WITHDRAW- TO BE LEFT ALONE
                (INTROVERTED FORM)

THOSE FROM A **SOFTER** ENVIRONMENT TAKE TWO FORMS:
    A) **STAR** : SEEKS TO BE THE CENTER — TAKE THE STAGE
                (EXTROVERTED FORM)
    B) **CLINGING VINE**: SEEKS TO FIND SOMEONE TO
                DEPEND ON
                (INTROVERTED FORM)

EARLY ON WE SEE JESUS WRESTLING IN THE DESERT
    WITH THE TEMPTATION TO USE HIS POWER
    AND CHARISMA **OVER** OTHERS (**NERO**),
    RATHER THAN EM-POWER OR EN-SPIRIT OTHERS.
WE ALSO SEE TOWARD THE END IN GETHSEMANE,
    JESUS STRUGGLES WITH THE DESIRE TO TURN BACK,
    TO HIDE, TO GO HOME (**TURTLE**).
WE SEE JESUS SAYING, *"DON'T CALL ME GOOD, NO ONE IS
GOOD BUT GOD ALONE!"* TO REJECT THE DOMINANT
RIGHTEOUSNESS OF THE RELIGIOUS (**STAR**).

THIS DOESN'T GO AWAY FOR JESUS,
        OR FOR US...
        NOT **EVER!**

LET'S NOT PRETEND WE ARE "BEYOND" THIS
        IN OUR EVER "ASCENDING" JOURNEY.

OUR JOURNEY IS NOT ABOUT
        GETTING **BEYOND** THIS,
    BUT IN BECOMING MORE **AWARE, AND COURAGEOUS**
    IN FACING THIS "EMBARRASSING",
    BUT VERY GROUNDING, HUMBLING REALITY.

TO WRESTLE WITH THE "EGO-CENTRIC EGO"
    IS CENTRAL TO JESUS' SPIRITUALITY AND TO OURS.

TO CHOOSE TO BE UNCONSCIOUS OF THIS IS
    TO INVITE A PART OF US
    TO **REGULARLY SABOTAGE**
    OUR FINEST INTENTIONS AND EFFORTS.

SHADOW 201: "WOUNDS"

*"It is 1978.   my wounds are completely in my shadow.
 I have no awareness of this,
though I am suffering and others can see
 I am deeply troubled.
 I have a dream in which I am running
 down a road as if I am fine
('How are you?... I'm fine'... was our childhood mantra)
 But then I notice there is a large hole through my chest,
 and a trail of blood is running behind me on the road.
 However, I don't "see" it,
 since I am running busily on ahead."*

I HAD TO FACE MY HEART-WOUND.
    IT TOOK ME ON A LIFE-CHANGING JOURNEY.
    THE GOOD NEWS IS THAT THE WOUND IS THE PLACE
    WHERE WE ARE **OPEN TO THE WORLD**
        AND TO **ALL BEINGS AROUND US.**

JESUS WAS WOUNDED.
WAS IT THE PAIN OF LOSING HIS FATHER
    (OR OTHERS NOT KNOWING WHO HIS FATHER WAS),
    THAT INTENSIFIED HIS LONGING FOR GOD?
WAS IT THE OUTRAGE OF HIS MENTOR, JOHN, BEING
    ARRESTED, THEN MURDERED, THAT BROUGHT JESUS
    OUT INTO HIS "PUBLIC" WORK?

WAS IT THE WOUND OF HIS OWN FAMILY DECIDING
    HE HAD "LOST HIS MIND" THAT LED HIM INTO
    A NEW & EXPANDED "FAMILY"?

AND THEN THERE WERE.....
    THE MISUNDERSTANDINGS OF HIS OWN DISCIPLES,
    THE REJECTION BY RELIGIOUS LEADERS,
    THE HOSTILITY OF JERUSALEM AUTHORITIES,
    THE BETRAYALS OF JUDAS & PETER,
    THE ABANDONMENT OF HIS FRIENDS TOWARD THE END...
    AND THEN THERE WAS THE CRUCIFICTION:
        "MY GOD, MY GOD, WHY HAVE <u>YOU</u> FORSAKEN ME?

IN FACING THESE WOUNDS,
    JESUS OPENED TO THE WORLD'S PAIN
    AND BECAME TRULY
        "JESUS".

IN FACING OUR WOUNDS,
    WE OPEN AND BECOME TRULY
        "OURSELVES".

SHADOW 301: "THE DIVINE IMAGE"

"SO GOD CREATED HUMANKIND IN HIS IMAGE,
    IN THE IMAGE OF GOD
    HE CREATED THEM, MALE & FEMALE"   GENESIS 1:27

THIS IS THE ADVANCED COURSE IN THE "SHADOW".

<u>WHEREAS THE EGO-CENTRIC EGO LURKS SO NEAR,
    THE "IMAGE OF GOD" SEEMS SO REMOTE.
    IT TAKES A SPECIAL AWAKENING TO "SEE" THIS.</u>

IT WAS IN JOHN'S BAPTISM WHEN JESUS HEARD:
    "YOU ARE MY SON, THE BELOVED,
    IN YOU MAY SOUL TAKES DELIGHT."

JESUS WAS NEVER THE SAME.
    HE BEGAN TO "SEE HIMSELF" DIFFERENTLY AFTER THAT.
    HE HAD SOMETHING MUCH GREATER
    THAN HIS EGO NOW,
    AND IT WAS *IN* HIM.

THE IMAGE OF GOD IN HIM WAS
    A *CONNECTION* AND
    A *DESTINY*.
    IT NO LONGER WAS A CONCEPT OR A BELIEF.
    IT WAS A VORTEX OF ENERGY.

FOR ME THIS WAS LIKE UNEARTHING
    THE TREASURE HIDDEN IN THE FIELD (MATT. 13:44)
        (A GREAT SHADOW IMAGE).

THIS CREATED A REAL LONGING FOR GOD,
    A HOMESICKNESS LIKE THE YEARNING
        OF THE LOST, BEDRAGGLED SON OF LUKE 15
    FOR HIS FAMILY,
        HIS FATHER,
        HIS MOTHER,
        AND A PLACE
        AT THE FAMILY TABLE.

*"It is March 1965. I am 22 yr. old and a couple of weeks
into theological seminary.
I know already I'm not going to find what I need there,
but I am drawn to Rev. Martin Luther King.
He is an Baptist pastor who is caught up in a great movement for equality & justice. We are in
Selma, Alabama.
I am listening, watching him. He is about 13 yr. older,
but a light-year beyond me.
I am inspired, but afraid and hesitant.
He is strong and focused. There is something going on inside him that is helping him master
his fear and free him into a powerful outward life. He is a Christ-figure on a luminous journey
to a sure and untimely death.
Is this what the "New Human" looks like...?
His face, gentle, yet set like flint, in this march toward Montgomery remains with me."*

THE JOURNEY OF JESUS BEGINS WITH THE INWARD LIFE
AND FLOWERS INTO HIS OUTWARD JOURNEY.
THE OUTWARD JOURNEY STIMULATES & CHALLENGES
HIS INWARD LIFE AND SO THEY NOURISH &
ENERGIZE EACH OTHER.
IF THE INWARD JOURNEY IS THE
ROOT SYSTEM IN A DARK , MOIST SOIL,
THEN THE GREEN SHOOT HUNGRY FOR THE SUN,
LIFTING UPWARD, IS THE OUTWARD JOURNEY.

THE OUTWARD JOURNEY BEGINS WITH THE CALL OF GOD TO JESUS:

*"EMBODY/ ENACT THE REIGN OF GOD!
AND <u>NOT IN HEAVEN</u>.... HERE ON EARTH!"*
(SEE LORD'S PRAYER)

I SEE THE OUTWARD JOURNEY OF JESUS
UNFOLDING IN THE GOSPELS IN **FOUR WAYS**:

<u>I JESUS FINDS HIS VOICE</u>

*"AFTER JOHN WAS ARRESTED, JESUS WENT INTO GALILEE.
THERE HE PROCLAIMED THE GOOD NEWS FROM GOD SAYING,
'IT IS KAIROS'" (TIME TO AWAKEN)   MARK 1:14*

JOHN, HIS MENTOR, WAS SILENCED. JESUS STEPPED UP AND
SPOKE OUT. HE WAS NOW OUT IN THE PUBLIC WITH ALL IT'S PERIL

AND POSSIBILITY. IT ALSO SHOWS HOW **_CREATIVE_** ANGER AND
GRIEF **CAN** BE, IF SUBJECT TO THE CALL OF GOD.

II JESUS CALLS TOGETHER THE "NEW COMMUNITY"

THIS WAS THE 1ST PROTOTYPE...
WHAT THE REIGN OF GOD ACTUALLY LOOKED LIKE
    AMONG PEOPLE ...HERE & NOW.
SEE BELOW, PART A, "THE TABLE OF JESUS".

III JESUS TEACHES THE RADICAL VALUES OF THE REIGN OF GOD.

HE USES EARTHY IMAGES
    OF SALT,
        LIGHT ,
            SEED, AND
                LEAVEN.

(SALT) * RADICAL HOSPITALITY*

"YOU ARE SALT FOR THE EARTH..." MATTHEW 5:13

NO UP OR DOWN, NO IN OR OUT, NO US OR THEM,
NO HIERARCHY, SOCIAL CLASS...
CODES OF PURITY OR CONVENTION
    DISSOLVE IN THIS ATMOSPHERE.
NEW VALUE IS REVEALED FOR WOMEN, CHILDREN,
    SLAVES, OUTCASTS, THE POOR, CRIMINALS,
    PAGANS, AND OTHER SPECIES.
THEY **BECOME** THE SALT THAT
    SPICES UP THIS MOVEMENT.
THEY ARE THE "GUMBO" IN A
    FORMERLY "BLAND" RELIGIOUS SOUP.
    IT "TASTES" DIFFERENT.

(LIGHT) * COMPASSION TOWARD ALL*

*"YOU ARE LIGHT FOR THE WORLD... NO ONE LIGHTS A LAMP
TO PUT IT UNDER A TUB, THEY PUT IT ON A LAMPSTAND WHERE
IT SHINES FOR EVERYONE IN THE HOUSE..."*   MATT. 5: 14F.

RATHER THAN FOCUS ON LOVING ONE'S FRIENDS
    AND DOING CHARITY TOWARD THE NEEDY,
    THE FOCUS WAS ON **_BECOMING_** COMPASSIONATE.

NOT JUST DOING COMPASSIONATE ACTS,
   BUT **EMBODYING** COMPASSION.
THIS WAS A LIGHT THAT SHONE LIKE
   THE SUN ON EVERYONE AROUND...
A **STATE OF BEING** THAT BROUGHT
FORGIVENESS TO EVERYONE,
NON-VIOLENCE IN CONFLICT,
AND LOVE TO
      EVEN
         ONE'S ENEMIES.

(SEED) * Unimagined Power*
"THE REIGN OF GOD IS LIKE A TINY SEED..." MARK 4:31

WE SURRENDER TO THE BELOVED
   AND LIKE A SEED WE BECOME AN **OFFERING**
   THAT IN THE DARK AND MYSTERIOUS SOIL,
   ROOTS AND SPROUTS, BECOMING SOMETHING
   FAR BEYOND WHAT IT WAS, OR EVEN
   WHAT IT COULD IMAGINE.
   CAN THE ACORN IMAGINE THE OAK?
   CAN THE OLD HUMAN IMAGINE THE "NEW"?

(LEAVEN) * Sacred Subversion*
*"THE REIGN OF GOD...IS LIKE THE LEAVEN A WOMAN TOOK
AND MIXED IN WITH THREE MEASURES OF FLOUR TILL IT
WAS LEAVENED ALL THROUGH.."* LUKE 13:21

THE SMALL HIDDEN PRESENCE OF THE LEAVEN
   MYSTERIOUSLY TRANSFORMS THE WHOLE LOAF.
THE REIGN OF GOD MOVES NOT LIKE AN ARMY OR
   RULES OVER YOU LIKE AN EMPIRE,
   BUT ***SUBVERTS WITH SMALL ACTS OF
   INTEGRITY & COURAGE AND A SUBTLE,
   BUT LUMINOUS CREATIVE PRESENCE.***

NOTE THE IMPACT OF THE "SUBTLE" ACT OF
   FORGIVENESS OF THE MILKMAN WHO
   MURDERED CHILDREN WITHIN THE AMISH
   PENNSYLVANIA COMMUNITY IN 2006.
   A SMALL ACT IMPACTED THE WORLD.
   (VERY LEAVEN-LIKE)

IV BECOMING A CHANNEL OF DIVINE GRACE

THIS IS THE **2ND PROTOTYPE** OF THE REIGN OF GOD:
"THE **NEW HUMAN**".
THE DIVINE GRACE SEEKS TO BREAK
INTO THE WORLD OF HUMANS.
IT NEEDS AN INSTRUMENT, A FLUTE.
IT NEEDS A BODY TO BRING HEALING,
EMPOWERMENT, VISION, AND A CHALLENGE.
IT NEEDS AN HUMAN BEING WILLING TO BE MOLDED &
SHAPED ON THE WHEEL BY A POTTER
WITH A VISION AND A GRACIOUS SKILL.
THIS POTTER IS LOOKING FOR A WILLING VOLUNTEER.
THIS INSTRUMENT MAKER HAS MUSIC
THAT **NEEDS TO BE HEARD**.
SEE BELOW PART B, THE NEW HUMAN

THE 1ST PROTOTYPE: THE TABLE OF JESUS

"It is 1998. This Sunday morning I announce that everyone is welcome to come to "Holy Communion", since it is not "my" table, it is the table of "Jesus". I notice a woman who is struggling with crack cocaine does not come up.
After the service, I say she could have had "Communion" with everyone else. She says with tears, ' You mean you would have me...'?"

" *NOW WHILE HE WAS AT TABLE IN THE HOUSE,*
IT HAPPENED THAT A NUMBER OF TAX COLLECTORS
AND SINNERS CAME TO SIT AT THE TABLE WITH JESUS
AND HIS DISCIPLES.
WHEN THE PHARISEES SAW THIS,
THEY SAID TO HIS DISCIPLES,
'WHY DOES YOUR MASTER EAT WITH
TAX COLLECTORS AND SINNERS?
WHEN HE HEARD THIS HE REPLIED,
'IT IS NOT THE HEALTHY WHO NEED THE DOCTOR,
BUT THE SICK.
GO AND LEARN THE MEANING OF THE WORDS:
'MERCY IS WHAT PLEASES ME, NOT SACRIFICE'".   MATT. 9:10F.

*"The tax collectors and sinners, however,
were all crowding around to listen to him
and the Pharisees and Scribes complained saying,
'This man welcomes sinners and eats with them.'"*

Luke 15: 1f.

The table of Jesus is the 1st prototype,
an enactment/visual representation/
embodiment of the reign of God.
The table of Jesus welcomes the outcast &
privileged, the wounded & strong, rich & poor,
slave & master, Jew & gentile (pagan)...
All sit together, none higher or lower,
bound together by their "hunger".
There is food shared.
Young fresh faces, dark & light,
luminous wrinkled faces...
all join in table laughter, stories
& conversation, meeting of new friends.
It is a microcosm of the dream of God for humanity.
The dream had been shattered by violence,
injustice, hatred, prejudice, and war.
The dream was remembered at the table of Jesus.
The table of Jesus is the architect's drawing
for the healing of the world.
God was calling everyone back to
the **GREAT TABLE** with this table of Jesus.
We are called to **re-enact this vision**
at the church's table, our neighborhood's table,
and our **OWN** table in our homes.
This is what the reign of God looks like!

"When you have a feast, invite the poor, maimed, blind, and lame" Jesus in Luke 14:13

The table of Jesus is leaven transforming
the division and injustice of the world.
The table of Jesus brings together people
who would ordinarily **NEVER EAT**
with each other, or..... **EVEN MEET**.
The estranged meet,
eat,
and become a kind of new & greater family:
a sign of the **BREAKING IN OF SPIRIT** into
our weary & broken culture.
THIS IS THE REIGN OF GOD!

THE TABLE OF JESUS CHALLENGES
    OUR SPIRITUALITY AND SOUL.
    IT FORCES US TO FACE OUR SHADOWED
    ATTITUDES OF PRIVILEGE, OUR ARROGANCE,
    OUR JUDGMENT OF THOSE DIFFERENT.
    IT ESPECIALLY FORCES US TO **FACE OUR FEARS**.

WE MUST TRANSFORM TO STAY AT THIS TABLE.

WE DON'T NEED TO TRANSFORM,
    IF WE **STAY AT THE OLD TABLE**
    WHERE ONLY THOSE WHO THINK, ACT,
    AND LOOK LIKE US ARE WELCOME.
    WE DON'T NEED THE SPIRITUALITY OF JESUS THERE.
    WE DON'T NEED THE RIVER OF GOD.

JESUS CLEARED OPEN THE **COURT OF THE GENTILES**
    IN THE JERUSALEM TEMPLE PREVENTING
    THOSE WHO WERE USING IT AS A SHORTCUT AND
    CHASING OUT THOSE SELLING ANIMALS FOR
    SACRIFICE THERE. HE CRIED OUT,

    "DOES NOT SCRIPTURE SAY: 'MY HOUSE WILL BE
    CALLED A HOUSE OF PRAYER FOR *ALL PEOPLES*".
        (ISAIAH 56:7)   MARK 11:17

THE JERUSALEM TEMPLE SEPARATED THE GENTILES,
    WOMEN, MEN, PRIESTS IN DISTINCT COURTS FOR
    PRAYER. EVERYONE HAD A PLACE IN THIS TEMPLE.
    (THAT'S WHY JESUS WAS ANGRY THAT THE PLACE OF
    THE GENTILES WAS BEING DESECRATED.)
    EVEN THE DIVINE WAS IN A DISTINCT "HOLY OF HOLIES"
    AT THE CENTER WHERE ONLY THE HIGH PRIEST
    DARED VENTURE ONCE A YEAR.

BUT AT THE TABLE OF JESUS THE DIVISIONS HAVE
    DISSOLVED AND THEY ARE **ALL TOGETHER HERE**.
    EVEN "ADONAI", THE DIVINE ONE,
    HAS LEFT THE "HOLY OF HOLIES"
    FOR A TIME AND MYSTERIOUSLY
    TAKEN A PLACE AT THIS TABLE.

THE 2ND PROTOTYPE: THE NEW HUMAN

"It is 1982 and David Panosh has done a stone lithograph of the "Christ Stained-Glass Window" (next page). Christ is coming out of the window in stages and becoming more realistic in each emergence. I am moved, though some are saying Jesus looks too human, or even too much like the artist. David says that at church, Jesus has become "real" to him." When people saw the 'real' Jesus, did they see the 'New Human'...? Did they become 'real'...? And did that move them into the new life....?

THE REIGN OF GOD BECOMES
   VISIBLE IN THE WORLD IN TWO WAYS:
   THE **NEW COMMUNITY (THE TABLE OF JESUS**)
   AND THE **NEW HUMAN**.

BOTH ARE GREAT CHALLENGES THAT STRETCH US
   EMOTIONALLY, PHYSICALLY, AND SPIRITUALLY.

THE NEW HUMAN IS AN EVOLUTION,
   A LEAP IN THE LONG JOURNEY OF THE HUMAN SPECIES.
THIS IS NOT A "**GOOD**" HUMAN OR A "**PERFECT**" HUMAN
   BUT A "**NEW**" HUMAN: BROKEN & BEAUTIFUL,
   A SPIRIT-PERSON WHO HAS BECOME
   AN INSTRUMENT OF DIVINE GRACE.

JESUS BECOMES THE CHRIST:
   A PROTOTYPE OF THE NEW HUMAN,
   THE FULFILLMENT OF THE **DIVINE IMAGE** IN WHICH
   WE ARE **ALL** CREATED.

HE CALLS US TO **FOLLOW** AND
               BECOME THIS NEW HUMAN.

HE GAVE HIMSELF TO THIS CALLING.

SOME *CHARACTERISTICS* OF THE **NEW HUMAN** ARE:

1) FEARLESS *SELF-AWARENESS* TO FACE EGO-CENTRISM AND THE IMPAIRMENT OF OUR WOUNDS

2) *INTIMACY WITH GOD* TO OVERCOME EMPTY RELIGION & RITUAL AND GROUND US IN DIVINE PRESENCE & GRACE

3) *CREATION-CENTERED WORLD-VIEW* TO COMBAT EXCLUSIVE/TRIBAL RELIGION AND ALLOW AN EMBRACE OF THE WHOLE CREATION

4) *FREE & CREATIVE SPIRIT* TO WARD OFF AUTHORITARIAN RELIGION AND THE MOMENTUM OF TRADITION

5) *COMPASSION* THAT CHALLENGES THE URGE TO DOMINATE, REJECT, ABUSE

6) *NON-VIOLENCE* TO REPLACE TENDENCY TO REVENGE AND INCLINATION TO WAR

7) *ETHICAL WRESTLING* VALUED OVER STRICT MORALISM AND LEGALISM

8) *RICHNESS OF SOUL* INSTEAD OF THE "WEALTH" OF ACCUMULATIONS & MONEY

9) *WISDOM* TO BALANCE THE GIFT OF IMAGINATION & CREATIVITY AND REIGN IN AMBITION

HUMAN HISTORY HAS BLESSED US WITH GREAT EXAMPLES OF THIS **NEW HUMAN**:

FRANCIS OF ASSISI, MARY MAGDALENE, TERESA OF AVILA, RUMI, HILDEGARD OF BINGEN, CATHERINE OF SIENNA, GHANDI, MARTIN LUTHER KING JN., THICH NHAT HANH, MOTHER THERESA, DIETRICH BONHOEFFER, ABRAHAM HESCHEL, THE DALAI LAMA, RABIA, THOMAS MERTON, TAGORE ...   TO NAME JUST A FEW.

MY SOUL'S DESIRE IS TO BE THE
NEW HUMAN

YET, SOMETIMES
i HAVE SETTLED INTO
BEING THE "NICE BOY"
OF MY CHILDHOOD,

THE "GOOD CITIZEN"
OF MY CULTURE

OR THE "COMPETENT PASTOR"
OF MY PROFESSIONAL
LIFE

"It is 1978. I have been a pastor for 9 years.
My life is a mess: my marriage, my work, my back is out, and I have no sanctity in me. Fueled by coffee,
I am a train off it's tracks. I am haunted. I desperately go
on a silent retreat with Conrad Hoover. I pack books, guitar, and cross-country skiis, but I am left to myself in
the silence. I don't know how to pray. I try the Lord's Prayer, but feel nothing. Even that has abandoned me.
There is something there so vital for me, but I don't know how to get to it. How could this be so important to so many, and seem so empty to me? I take up a journal I just bought. It was a little brown booklet used for college tests... and I <u>am</u> being tested. A wrenching lostness pours out of me
and drenches that tiny book with anguish..."

THE LORD'S PRAYER CONTAINS THE SPIRITUALITY OF JESUS
   IN A PROFOUND WAY.
EACH PETITION OPENS ONE TO
   ANOTHER SPIRITUAL DIMENSION AND
   DRAWS ONE INTO A DEEP MEDITATION.
EACH ONE CAN LEAD INTO A LIFE-SHAPING PRACTICE.

WE BEGIN WITH A ***TRADITIONAL LORD'S PRAYER***, A 1989
   NEW REVISED STANDARD VERSION (NRSV) TRANSLATED
   FROM THE GREEK MANUSCRIPTS. GREEK WAS THE
   LANGUAGE OF THE WRITERS OF THE GOSPELS IN THE
   CHRISTIAN BIBLE.

THEN WE LOOK AT A POSSIBLE ***TRANSLATION FROM ARAMAIC***
   RENDERINGS. I HAVE DRAWN UPON THE TRANSLATIONS
   OF NEIL DOUGLAS-KLOTZ & GEORGE LAMSA. [5]
   ARAMAIC IS AN ANCIENT & POETIC LANGUAGE LIKE
   HEBREW AND ARABIC WHICH THE HEBREWS LEARNED IN
   EXILE, AND WAS THE LANGUAGE SPOKEN BY JESUS AND
   HIS DISCIPLES. THERE ARE MANY POSSIBILITIES IN
   TRANSLATING ARAMAIC, SO I AM GOING TO USE WHAT HAS
   EMERGED FOR ME IN **PRAYING** VERSIONS OF
   AN ARAMAIC LORD'S PRAYER FOR THE LAST 18 YEARS.
   THE PRAYER ACTUALLY FOUND ITS **OWN** VOICE.

THEN WE LOOK AT HOW I ALLOWED THIS
   ARAMAIC VERSION TO BE "EMBODIED" IN MY OWN BEING.
   IT WAS THEN THAT IT ENTERED ME WHOLLY, AND IT HAS NEVER LEFT.

1) "*Our Father In Heaven*"   (NRSV)

**"*O Divine Beloved, Your radiant presence shines
in all the universe*"**   (Aramaic version)

"Father" is a translation of the greek word,
"pater". And "pater" is a Greek attempt to
translate "Abba".
Jesus called the Divine, "Abba", which
was a term of intimate endearment beyond what the
word "father" can carry, especially for so
many who have had issues with their own personal fathers.
If we must translate, why not the intimate and dear,
"Divine Beloved"? In praying, it works.
There is a falling into the Holy One here.
And that's what Jesus is doing.

Embodiment:
    Arms outstretched, we pray words as we turn to the six
Directions: east, south, west, north, the sky above,
and then to the earth below.
(We are immersed in the Divine Beauty. The Lord's Prayer is
    esp. rich prayed out-of-doors, centered in the universe.)

2) "*Hallowed be your name*"   (NRSV)

"*I will hold your radiance & beauty in my heart*"
                  (Aramaic)

The Aramaic root word "Shem" carries meaning of "light,
radiance, name". We are drawing all the radiance of God's
Creation into the temple of our heart and are filled with
beauty and awe and wonder.

Embodiment:
    Bring hands together at heart, head bends down toward
heart, the inner temple, the 7th direction.

3) "*Your Kingdom come*"   (NRSV)

**"*Create your reign of shalom... here & now,
use these willing hands and this passionate heart*"**
                  (Aramaic)

This is a passionate cry for the breaking in of God's reign
right here in our midst.

JESUS UNDERSTANDS THAT THIS IS A CO-LABORATION,
A CO-CREATION BETWEEN THE DIVINE DESIRE
AND OUR WILLINGNESS TO SERVE.
THIS IS THE MOST DYNAMIC PARTNERSHIP THERE IS.
THE HEBREW WORD "SHALOM" CARRIES MEANINGS OF "WHOLENESS,
JUSTICE, RECONCILIATION, PEACE, UNITY".
ALL OF WHICH IS GOD'S GREAT LONGING FOR US.

EMBODIMENT:

OUTSTRETCHED ARMS PLEAD FOR GOD'S REIGN........
THEN IN OFFERING, OPEN HANDS ("USE THESE HANDS")
AND THEN THUMP HEART ("AND THIS PASSIONATE HEART")

4) *"YOUR WILL BE DONE , ON EARTH, AS IT IS IN HEAVEN"*
                                                    (NRSV)

"MAY YOUR HEART'S DESIRE BECOME MY HEART'S DESIRE, MAY THEY BE JOINED AS ONE"   (ARAMAIC)

HERE I PRAY THAT THE DIVINE DESIRE FOR "WHOLENESS,
JUSTICE, RECONCILIATION, PEACE, UNITY" MAY BECOME MY HEART'S
LONGING, AND EVEN MORE,
THEY MAY BECOME **ONE GREAT JOINED ENERGY**.

EMBODIMENT:

MY LEFT ARM REACHES UP, SYMBOLIZING THE DIVINE DESIRE.
MY RIGHT HAND IS AT MY HEART, SYMBOLIZING MY OWN DESIRES. I PRAY
THAT MY HEART IS SHAPED INTO THE DIVINE DESIRE FOR WHOLENESS,
JUSTICE, RECONCILIATION, PEACE, AND UNITY. AS I AM MOVED, MY
HANDS MOVE TOGETHER, UNTIL THEY JOIN IN FRONT OF ME, PALM TO
PALM, THEN CLASPING EACH OTHER. THIS IS THE SURRENDER OF THE
HEART TO THE DIVINE HEART AND A JOINING OF HEARTS.

5) *"GIVE US THIS DAY OUR DAILY BREAD"*   (NRSV)

"GRANT WHAT WE NEED EACH DAY IN BREAD & WISDOM"
                                                    (ARAMAIC)

THIS IS A PLEA TO BE FED FROM THE HAND OF GOD, TO BE SUSTAINED
WITH FOOD, BOTH PHYSICAL AND SPIRITUAL.
WE STARVE WITHOUT ***BOTH GIFTS OF GOD***. THIS
IS A TRANSITION IN THE PRAYER. THIS IS A BREAKING FORTH OF NEED &
GRATITUDE BEFORE WE TURN TOWARD THE DARK SIDE AND THE
STRUGGLE AHEAD IN THE PRAYER.

EMBODIMENT:

HANDS WHIRL UP FROM THE EARTH, BRINGING HER GIFTS, PALMS OPEN, FACING UP, RECEIVING BREAD IN ONE HAND, & WISDOM IN THE OTHER. BOTH ARE DIVINE GIFTS OF GRACE.

6) *"AND FORGIVE US OUR DEBTS, AS WE ALSO HAVE FORGIVEN OUR DEBTORS."*   (NRSV)

"RELEASE US FROM THE BURDEN OF OUR FAILURES, AS WE RELEASE THOSE WHO HAVE FAILED US."
                                                            (ARAMAIC)

LUKE'S VERSION OF THE LORD'S PRAYER HAS "SIN" INSTEAD OF "DEBT". THE ARAMAIC COULD BE "FAILURES". WE BEG TO BE FREE OF FAILURES THAT HAVE HAUNTED US, LIFE'S MISTAKES THAT WE HAVE HELD ONTO AND RE-SUFFERED OVER & OVER. BUT THE DEAL IS THAT **WE WILL LET GO OF OUR RESENTMENT AND ANGER TOWARD OTHERS** WHO HAVE DISAPPOINTED, HURT, FAILED US, AND EVEN "OWE DEBTS" TO US. WE REALIZE THESE ARE LIKE HOT COALS THAT WE HAVE STUBBORNLY HELD ONTO, WAY TOO LONG, CAUSING OUR OWN SUFFERING... THE PERVERSE PLEASURE OF ANGUISHED RELATIONSHIP.

EMBODIMENT:

ARMS CROSS TIGHTLY AROUND CHEST, THEN WHEN FEELING FREED FROM THESE FAILURES, ARMS MOVE OUTWARD... LEAVING ARMS OPEN, BUT FISTS ARE CLENCHED.
FISTS HOLD THOSE WHO HAVE FAILED US, AND ONLY OPEN UNTIL YOUR HEART IS READY TO LET GO OF THEM AND YOUR RESENTMENT/ANGER TOWARD THEM.
THEN HANDS ARE OPEN & EMPTY (AND USEFUL).

7) *"AND DO NOT BRING US TO THE TIME OF TRIAL"*   (NRSV)

"BREAK THE HOLD OF OUR DISTRACTIONS"   (ARAMAIC)

THE ARAMAIC IS SUGGESTIVE OF THAT WHICH WOULD SEDUCE US FROM OUR PATH. THERE ARE SO MANY DISTRACTIONS, OBSESSIONS, ADDICTIONS, SHOPPING, CONSUMERISM, AND JUST PLAIN OLD EGO-CENTRISM THAT CAN DRAW AWAY OUR FOCUS FROM OUR AUTHENTIC PATH, OUR SPIRITUAL JOURNEY.

EMBODIMENT:

WHILE FACING FORWARD, YOUR RIGHT HAND COMES AGAINST SIDE OF YOUR FACE AND PUSHES IT TO THE LEFT, AWAY FROM THE PATH BEFORE YOU, AND BLINDING YOUR WAY.

8) *"BUT RESCUE US FROM EVIL"* (NRSV)

"AND FREE US FROM THE FEARS THAT HOLD US BACK...
AND THE EVIL SO CLOSE" (ARAMAIC)

WHILE WE FOCUS ON OUR PATH BEFORE US , THERE IS FEAR THAT SURROUNDS IT. IT IS LIKE A VEIL BEFORE US KEEPING US IN OUR SAFE, BUT STUCK PLACE. WE PRAY FOR FREEDOM FROM THIS, AND REACH OUT TO OPEN THIS VEIL OF FEAR SO THAT WE CAN STEP AHEAD. AS WE TAKE THIS NEXT STEP, WE NOTICE OUR FISTS ARE BEHIND US. THE POTENTIAL OF EVIL ALWAYS GOES WITH US AND IS ALWAYS BEHIND US AND *OUT OF VIEW*. WE AVOID EVIL AS MUCH AS HUMANLY POSSIBLE. AND WHEN WE DO CONFRONT EVIL, IT IS USUALLY THE EVIL "OUT THERE".
THAT CAN LEAD TO ALL KINDS OF DESTRUCTIVE RESPONSES.
JESUS WOULD LEAD US DEEPER INTO THE *POTENTIAL EVIL* IN WHICH WE ARE COMPLICIT, YET BLIND TO.
AMERICANS FOUGHT IN WWII TO STOP THE EVIL OF THE THIRD REICH AND THE JAPANESE EMPIRE, BUT WERE UNABLE TO SEE THE EVIL OF THE DETENTIONS OF JAPANESE-AMERICANS IN AMERICA, OR THE RACIAL SEGREGATION IN AMERICA IN THE 1940'S.

EMBODIMENT:
HANDS MOVE FORWARD TO GRASP VEIL OF FEAR IN FRONT OF YOU, AS YOU IMAGE THE NEXT STEP ON YOUR JOURNEY. WHEN READY, YOU OPEN VEIL WITH BOTH HANDS AND PULL IT ROUND AND BEHIND YOU AS YOU TAKE THE NEXT STEP FORWARD WITH BOTH FEET.
HANDS MOVE AS FISTS AROUND YOUR BODY AND REMAIN BEHIND YOUR BODY REPRESENTING THE POTENTIAL OF EVIL ALWAYS THERE, BUT HIDDEN FROM VIEW.

9) *"FOR THE KINGDOM, AND THE POWER, AND THE GLORY,*
ARE YOURS FOREVER. AMEN." (NRSV)

"FOR YOURS IS THE REIGN OF SHALOM, THE POWER, AND THE SONG
FROM AGE TO AGE. AMEN. IT IS SEALED IN TRUST"
(ARAMAIC)

THIS IS A CELEBRATION OF THE DIVINE ONE WHO HAS IMAGINED, CREATED, RE-CREATED, SUSTAINED ALL LIFE WITH GRACE AND LOVING ATTENTION THROUGH DIVINE POWER AND THE MUSIC OF THE SOUL THROUGH ALL GENERATIONS. THIS PRAYER IS A SACRED AND INTIMATE TRUST BETWEEN OUR SOUL AND THE DIVINE SOUL.

EMBODIMENT:
    ARMS EXTEND (YOURS IS THE REIGN...)
HANDS COME TOGETHER, ALMOST MEET,
    AT SOLAR PLEXIS (THE POWER)
HANDS RISE UP TOGETHER AS IF SONG
    WAS BEING RELEASED (AND THE SONG)
HANDS LOWER ON EACH SIDE...
    CARVING A LARGE CIRCLE (FROM AGE TO AGE)
HANDS COME UP,
    REST AT HEART. (AMEN. IT IS SEALED IN TRUST)

NOW PUT IT ALL TOGETHER AND PRAY

THE ARAMAIC LORD'S PRAYER

WITH THE MOVEMENTS AND

YOUR WHOLE BEING

WILL <u>BECOME</u> THIS PRAYER,

AND YOUR BODY WILL "<u>GET</u>"

THE SPIRITUALITY OF JESUS.

An Aramaic Lord's Prayer   The Embodiment

"O Divine Beloved,	Arms stretch out in embrace
Your Radiant Presence Shines In all the Universe	Face the 6 Directions (E,S,W,N, Sky, Earth)
I will hold your Radiance & Beauty in my heart	Hands hold 7th Direction (the Temple of the Heart)
Create your Reign of Shalom NOW... (use these willing hands & this passionate heart)	Arms extend in passionate URGENCY ... stretch hands out... THUMP HEART IN OFFERING
May your heart's desire become mine... May they be joined as ONE	One hand up, other at heart Hands come together, clasp
Grant what we need each day In bread & wisdom	Hands whirl up from earth, receiving one in each hand
Release us from the burden of Our failures... as we release Those who have failed us.	Arms tight around chest, arms release & open. When able to let go... fists unclench & open
Break the hold of our distractions	Hand pushes face to side, blinding our path
And free us from the fears that hold us back...	Hands pull away curtain, opens path, step forward
...& the evil so close	Hands closed, behind self
For yours is the reign of shalom, the power, and the Song, from age to age AMEN. It is sealed in trust	Arms extend out Hands to solar plexis, hands rise together above Hands lower, carve circle Hands up, rest at heart

THE SPIRITUALITY OF JESUS IN PSALM 23 (THE "OTHER" LORD'S PRAYER)

PSALM 23	THE GOSPELS OF JESUS
"THE LORD IS MY SHEPHERD I SHALL NOT BE IN WANT	"SET YOUR HEART ON GOD'S REIGN, AND ALL THESE OTHER THINGS WILL BE GIVEN YOU AS WELL" MATT.6:33
HE MAKES ME LIE DOWN IN GREEN PASTURES	"MEDITATE ON THE BIRDS IN THE SKY, ON FLOWERS GROWING... MATT.6:26
AND LEADS ME BESIDES STILL WATERS	"JESUS SPENT THE WHOLE NIGHT IN PRAYER TO GOD" LUKE 6:12
HE RESTORES MY SOUL, AND GUIDES ME ALONG RIGHT PATHWAYS FOR HIS NAME'S SAKE	"LOVE THE LORD YOUR GOD WITH ALL YOUR HEART, SOUL, MIND... AND A 2ND IS LIKE IT: LOVE YOUR NEIGHBOR AS YOURSELF..." MATT. 22:37
THOUGH I WALK THROUGH THE VALLEY OF THE SHADOW OF DEATH I SHALL FEAR NO EVIL, FOR YOU ARE WITH ME;	"JESUS KNEW THAT "ABBA" HAD PUT EVERYTHING INTO HIS HANDS, AND THAT HE HAD COME FROM GOD, & WAS RETURNING TO GOD, HE ROSE FROM THE TABLE" JN.13:3
YOUR ROD & YOUR STAFF, THEY COMFORT ME.	"AND ANGELS APPEARED, AND MINISTERED TO (JESUS)" MT. 4:11
YOU PREPARE A TABLE BEFORE ME IN THE PRESENCE OF MY ENEMIES	*CEREMONY OF CONSECRATION* I AM CHOSEN — TABLE SET BEFORE ME IN MIDST OF MY CHAOS & CONFLICT
YOU ANOINT MY HEAD WITH OIL	I AM ANOINTED (HEBREW: MASHACH MEANS "CHRISTED"/ "SET APART")
AND MY CUP IS RUNNING OVER	"AS ABBA SENT ME, SO I AM SENDING YOU. HE BREATHED ON THEM... RECEIVE THE HOLY RUACH (BREATH, SPIRIT, WIND)" JOHN 20:21
SURELY YOUR GOODNESS & MERCY SHALL FOLLOW ME	"ASK, AND IT WILL BE GIVEN TO YOU" MATT. 7:7
ALL THE DAYS OF MY LIFE & I WILL DWELL IN THE HOUSE OF THE LORD FOREVER."	JESUS PRAYS: "AND WE WILL COME TO YOU AND MAKE A HOME (DWELLING /TEMPLE) IN YOU" JOHN 14:23

REFLECTIONS ON PSALM 23

PSALM 23 IS THE MOST BELOVED PSALM TO MANY.
BUT IT ALSO CONVEYS SO CLEARLY
 THE SPIRITUALITY OF JESUS.
THE PSALM IS DIVIDED BY LINES ABOVE INTO THREE PARTS.

THE **1ST THIRD** FOCUSES ON THE CARE, PROTECTION, AND HEALING PRESENCE OF THE DIVINE.

THE **2ND THIRD** IS MORE PERSONAL, SHIFTING FROM THE THIRD PERSON "HE" TO THE SECOND PERSON "YOU". IT ALSO INTENSIFIES TO A MORE INTIMATE & FIERCE PROTECTION, AKIN TO A MOTHER BEAR FOR HER CUB.

THE **LAST THIRD** RETAINS THE 2ND PERSON BUT IS SET IN CEREMONY.
THE DIVINE ACTIVELY CREATES
    A **CEREMONY DESIGNED FOR YOU.**
THIS INCLUDES THE PREPARATION OF THE CEREMONIAL TABLE (ALTAR),
THEN A CONSECRATION.
THE CONSECRATION IS A SETTING APART ONE'S LIFE FOR A CALLING.
TO ANOINT (HEBREW: MASHACH) CARRIES THE SAME MEANING AS THE WORD "CHRIST".
SO THIS IS A "CHRISTING" CEREMONY IN WHICH ONE IS INVITED TO SHARE IN THE GREAT WORK OF GOD.
(JESUS EXPERIENCED THIS HIMSELF AND
    CONSECRATED HIS FOLLOWERS BREAD, BREATH, AND BODY.)

THIS IS A **SACRED PARTNERSHIP.**
THIS RAISES THE ANTE OF ONE'S LIVING TO A NEW LEVEL.
THIS IS SUCH A GIFT, SO UNEXPECTED,
    THAT EVEN ONE'S FEELING OF UNWORTHINESS IS LEFT BEHIND
    (HOPEFULLY).
THIS IS MORE THAN ANCIENT MIDDLE- EASTERN HOSPITALITY HERE.
IT IS IS AN IMMENSE BLESSING
    TO BE SO SEEN BY GOD...
    SO VALUED... ESTEEMED THAT ONE RESPONDS:
"MY CUP IS RUNNING OVER".

**SURELY AFTER THIS, WHAT CAN HAPPEN TO ME
THAT WOULD SHAKE MY SPIRITUAL INFRASTRUCTURE**?

IT IS LIKE LIVING IN THE **TEMPLE OF THE BELOVED**
    FOR THE REST OF MY DAYS, AND EVEN TO HAVE THE TEMPLE
    FIRMLY ROOTED IN MY OWN SOUL.
SINCE THIS IS SO FULL OF VIVID IMAGES THAT ARE
 MEANT TO BE TAKEN INTO ONE'S PSYCHE,
 I INVITE YOU TO SAY EACH PHRASE
AND "IMAGE" IT IN YOUR IMAGINATION.

(IF IT HELPS, NOW THAT YOU UNDERSTAND THE SHIFT
 FROM THE "HE" TO THE "YOU" AFTER THE 1ST PART,
 YOU CAN CHANGE THE "HE" TO "YOU" IN THE 1ST PART.
 IT CAN BE HELPFUL TO MANY TO ESCAPE THE MASCULINE IMAGE).

MEMORIZING IT HELPS, AS IT THEN FLOWS IN ONE PIECE.
THIS IS AN HEALING & EMPOWERING MEDITATION TO RETURN TO.
IT IS ESPECIALLY POWERFUL TO OPEN TO THE WORDS
     ONE <u>MIGHT HEAR</u> AS YOU ARE BEING ANOINTED.

<u>ENACT THE CEREMONY</u>.

Take some sacred oil and place it on your forehead.

   Can you feel the Grace?

   Do you hear the words of mercy

      whispered in YOUR inward ear?

Listen deeply............

FOR WHEN WE <u>FEEL THE GRACE AND</u>

      <u>HEAR THOSE WORDS</u>

       <u>AND RESPOND</u>,

IT IS OUR HEART'S DELIGHT,

EVEN IF IT IS VERY CHALLENGING.

EXPECT SOME CHALLENGE...
              THAT'S WHEN IT GETS GOOD.

EXPECT HEALING TOO, THEY GO TOGETHER.

<u>PSALM 23 AND THE LORD'S PRAYER</u>
   COMPLEMENT EACH OTHER WELL AND
   MAKE A POWERFUL PRAYER PRACTICE TOGETHER.

CHAPTER III THE PRACTICE OF JESUS' SPIRITUALITY

ON THE FOLLOWING PAGE IS AN ARTWORK TITLED "THE DOORS".
ARTISTS & MUSICIANS EXPRESS WHAT WORDS CAN'T SAY.
THEY CARRY THE MEANINGS OF "SPIRITUALITY",
WHEN WE HAVE LOST THE LANGUAGE FOR IT.

HERE MARK JOHN HOFFMAN LAYS IN FRONT OF OUR CHURCH BUILDING
AND SEES SOMETHING "MORE".
THERE ARE THE CHURCH DOORS, THE ENTRY PLACE.
BUT AS YOUR EYES RISE, THE STRUCTURE SWAYS AS IF
TO MOVE YOU AWAY FROM ITSELF.
THIS IS LIKE THE POINTER STARS OF THE GREAT MOTHER BEAR
POINTING TOWARD POLARIS, THE NORTH STAR. IT SWIRLS YOU UP
INTO THE COSMOS AND THE SPIRAL GALAXY WE LIVE WITHIN AND
PULLS YOU TOWARD THE IMAGE OF THE COSMIC HOLY ONE,
THE DIVINE BELOVED AT THE CENTER OF EVERYTHING THAT IS.

IS THIS THE BUILDING IN "WORSHIP"?
IS THIS THE BUILDING LAYING ASIDE IT'S "EGO" AND HISTORY?

ALSO, ABOVE AN IMAGE OF THE EARTH, A HUMAN FIGURE IS REACHING
UP IN A KIND OF DANCE IN CELEBRATION AND LONGING FOR
THE DIVINE. THE HUMAN IS JOINED BY A WOLF-LIKE ANIMAL AND
DOVE AND OTHER LIFE-FORMS IN THIS SACRED DANCE OF THE DIVINE
IN THE COSMOS. THE CHURCH EVEN JOINS THE ANIMALS AND THE
HUMAN IN THIS CEREMONY OF "INTERBEING"*.
THERE IS RHYTHM & MUSIC HERE TOO, YOU CAN FEEL THE PULSE,
A KIND OF HOLY HEART-BEAT THAT EVERYTHING SEEMS
TO BE MOVING WITH.

IS THIS WHAT JESUS WAS CALLING US INTO...?
TO COME OUT OF OUR SACRED BUILDINGS
INTO THE COSMOS OF THE BELOVED,
TO SEE THAT THE "DOORS" ARE A ENTRY TO SOMETHING
WAY BEYOND ITSELF, THE "REIGN OF GOD"...
TO SEE THAT IS WAS A PARTICIPATION, NOT JUST A MEDITATION...
TO SEE THAT IT WAS ABOUT THE WHOLE CREATION, NOT JUST "US"...
TO SEE THAT IT COULDN'T BE CONTAINED WITHIN THE DOORS...
TO SEE THAT IT WAS MORE A DANCE THAN A CREED...
TO SEE THAT IT WAS A WAY OF BEING, NOT JUST A WAY OF BELIEVING..
TO SEE THAT IT WAS A *PRACTICE*....

*(A WORD COINED BY THICH NHAT HANH)

JESUS IS VERY CLEAR...

"THEREFORE, EVERYONE
     WHO LISTENS TO THESE WORDS OF MINE
     AND ACTS ON THEM WILL BE LIKE THE SENSIBLE ONE
     WHO BUILT THEIR HOUSE ON ROCK.
     RAIN CAME...FLOODS ROSE, GALES BLEW...
      BUT IT DID NOT FALL:
      IT WAS FOUNDED ON ROCK"

MATT. 7:24

JESUS' SPIRITUALITY IS VERY INTERESTING TO STUDY,
     I'VE BEEN DOING IT FOR 44 YEARS.
     BUT IF YOU PRACTICE IT,
     YOU FIND YOUR LIFE CHANGING.
     YOU TAKE ON THE CHARACTERISTICS OF THAT LIGHT,
     SALT, SEED, AND LEAVEN THAT JESUS TALKS ABOUT.

TO DO THIS ALONE AS A PERSON IS
                    TRANSFORMING & LUMINOUS.

BUT IF A GROUP, OR CONGREGATION
     PRACTICES THIS TOGETHER,
     YOU HAVE A SPIRIT-MOVEMENT
          THAT CAN BRING HEALING,
            OPEN THE EYES OF THE BLIND
              & THE EARS OF THE DEAF.
     IT CAN CAUSE A SEISMIC SHIFT IN A CULTURE.
     IT ACCESSES THE ENERGIES OF GOD.

SO BEGIN WITH THE PRACTICES
     AND SHARE YOUR EXPERIENCES
     AND SUPPORT THOSE WHO ARE JOINING YOU.

OR IF YOU ARE ALONE,
     FIND A FRIEND OR COMPANION TO SHARE YOUR JOURNEY.
     DISCOVER WHAT CAN HAPPEN.
     THERE IS NO MORE AMAZING ADVENTURE.

THE PRACTICE OF JESUS" SPIRITUALITY:

TO HEAL & CHANGE THE HEART

LUB DUB....LUB DUB...LUB DUB...LUB DUB...LUB DUB...LUB DUB...LUB DUB...

TO HEAL & CHANGE THE WORLD

LUB DUB...LUB DUB...   LUB DUB...LUB DUB

ALL THE PRACTICES OF JESUS ARE DOORWAYS & ENTRY PLACES INTO JESUS' SPIRITUALITY AND THE NEW BEING

THE 1ST PRACTICE: THE DAILY MEETING

HILDEGARD OF BINGEN (1098-1179) WAS AWAKENED FROM A
SYMBOLIC "SLEEP" IN HER MIDDLE YEARS INTO A NEW CREATIVE, FIERY
LIVING. SHE HEARS...

*"O HUMAN BEING, WHY DO YOU SLEEP...
WHY DO YOU NOT SEARCH OUT THE
HOUSE OF YOUR HEART?"* [6]

WE BEGIN HERE WITH THE DAILY MEETING,
ENTERING THE "HOUSE OF THE HEART",
BECAUSE IT WAS SO FOUNDATIONAL TO JESUS.
JESUS HAD REGULAR MEETINGS
WITH HIS OWN SOUL & WITH GOD...
OR IS IT THE SAME THING?
MEISTER ECKHART SAID THE GROUND OF THE SOUL
& THE GROUND OF GOD **WERE** THE SAME. [2]

JESUS GOES INTO THE DESERT...
HE GOES OFF INTO THE NIGHT...
HE STAYS OUT ALL NIGHT ALONE...
HE DISAPPEARS INTO THE DAWN...
HE OFTENS GOES AWAY ALONE...

THE DISCIPLES HE GATHERED DO NOT SEEM
TO UNDERSTAND HIS INWARD JOURNEY,
AND IT SHOWS IN THEIR
"UNCONSCIOUSNESS" ABOUT THEMSELVES.

HE TEACHES THEM TO GO INTO A CLOSET
AND THERE LEARN TO PRAY IN SECRET, IN THE DARKNESS.
THEY CAN'T READ THERE, IF THEY COULD READ.
THEY CAN ONLY LEARN HOW TO PRAY
& READ THE BOOK OF THEIR OWN SOUL.

HE TELLS THEM TO BECOME LIKE THE
RAVENS OF THE AIR
OR THE FLOWERS OF THE FIELD
TO RELIEVE THEIR ANXIETY
AND FALL INTO BEING... AND...
PRESENCE.

HE TRIES TO BRING THEM ALONG TO EXPERIENCE
    SOLITUDE, MEDITATION, AND PRAYER.

HE TAKES THEM TO A LONELY PLACE TOGETHER.

HE TAKES 3 OF THEM UP A MOUNTAIN TO PRAY.

HE BRINGS THEM WITH HIM TO THE GARDEN OF
      GETHSEMANE TO BEG FOR THEIR PRAYER SUPPORT
      FOR HIMSELF BEFORE HE WILL BE TAKEN
      IN THE NIGHT BY THE ROMAN BRIGADE CLOSING IN.

IT IS A MAJOR THRUST OF JESUS' LIFE TO HAVE
    HIS SPIRITUAL COMMUNITY **LEARN TO PRAY...**
    & THUS EVOLVE...
    & BECOME A **TRANSFORMING MOVEMENT** IN THE WORLD.

SO WE TOO MUST BE INVITED INTO THIS PRACTICE.
    SO MUCH CAN BEGIN HERE.
    THERE ARE NO RULES, DEMANDS, STRUCTURE,
    MEMORIZED PRAYERS NECESSARY HERE.
IT IS SIMPLY A TIME APART, A DAILY MEETING.
THIS CAN HAPPEN ANYWHERE AND ANYTIME.
OUTSIDE IN NATURE IS GREAT,
      INSIDE IN A SPECIAL PLACE IS WONDERFUL.

I CLAIMED A LITTLE ROOM IN OUR HOME AND
    CREATED A SACRED SPACE WHERE I BEGIN EACH DAY.
    IT HAS ABSOLUTELY SAVED MY LIFE.

OUR SOUL CAN FEEL ABANDONED, IGNORED,
    EVEN A STRANGER TO US.
    OUR SOUL LOVES THIS MEETING.
    THE SOUL SAYS, **"AH, YOU DO CARE...**
        YOU HAVE COME HOME...
        YOU DO WANT TO KNOW ME, YOUR OWN TRUE SELF".
    AND SO THE FRIENDSHIP BEGINS.

AND GOD, WHO CAN FEEL AS **ABANDONED BY US**,
    LOVES THIS SPACE.
    GOD'S JOY IS PRESENCE & BLESSING & TRUTH.

    THE LAST WORD "TRUTH" CAN BE UNCOMFORTABLE,
    BUT WOULD YOU RATHER **NOT KNOW**?

HERE ARE SOME POSSIBILITIES FOR THE 1ST PRACTICE:
* WALKING PRAYER/MEDITATION IN THE PARK
* DEVOTIONAL READING OF SCRIPTURE
    & SILENT LISTENING
* YOGA & PRAYER / SILENCE
* AEROBICS/ DANCE FOLLOWED BY PRAYER/ SILENCE
* BODY PRAYER WITH MUSIC, THEN SILENCE
* DEVOTIONAL CHANT, THEN PRAYER/ SILENCE
* JOURNAL/ DREAM WRITING, THEN SILENCE
* PRAYING THROUGH A MUSICAL INSTRUMENT
* IMPROVISATIONAL SINGING / SOUND
* JUST BE LED BY THE SPIRIT & ALLOW WHATEVER

REMEMBER THAT ***SIMPLE, DEEP BREATHING***
    IS THE OLDEST/ FASTEST WAY TO SHIFT CONSCIOUSNESS
    AND MOVE INTO THE "PRAYER OF THE HEART".
    WE CENTER OURSELVES SO WE CAN LISTEN.
THE **CHALLENGE** OF THE 1ST PRACTICE IS
    TO OPEN UP THE TIME & SPACE IN OUR LIFE TO *DO* THIS.
    OUR LIVES CAN BE SO BUSY AND CROWDED THAT WE
    BECOME "EATEN" BY OUR CULTURE
    WHICH CALLS US TO BE "BUSY" TO HAVE MEANING.
    IT DOES NOT VALUE THE SOUL OR MINDFUL PRESENCE,
    AND REWARDS FRENETIC ACTIVITY AND MULTI-TRACKING.

AFTER SEVERAL MONTHS OF PRACTICING THE SIX PRACTICES OF
    JESUS' SPIRITUALITY AS A CONGREGATION, I ASKED THEM WHICH
    WAS THE HARDEST. THEY SAID IT WAS THE 1ST ONE, THE DAILY
    MEETING. IT SEEMED SO HARD TO FIND TIME, EVEN FOR
    RETIRED PEOPLE!
SO THIS MOVES AGAINST THE CURRENT
    AND REQUIRES A MUSCULAR EFFORT TO PUSH BACK
    AND AWAY SO WE CAN RECOVER
    SACRED TIME & SACRED SPACE.
THEN WE CAN BEGIN TO BREATHE AGAIN AND
    GIVE OUR HEART & ADRENAL GLANDS A BREAK.
    IN FACT, THE 100 BILLION NEURONS (BRAIN CELLS)
    IN OUR BRAIN CAN ALL RELAX. CELLS NEED SABBATH TOO.
    BEING A CELL IS A THANKLESS JOB.
    WHY NOT GIVE ALL 100 TRILLION HUMAN CELLS
        IN OUR BODY A REPRIEVE,
        WITHOUT HAVING TO DIE TO GET ONE.
        AFTER ALL, OUR CELLS *ARE* US.
THIS COULD BE THE MOST IMPORTANT THING YOU EVER DO.
IT WAS FOR ME. WHO CAN SAY WHAT CAN COME OF THIS?

REMEMBER WHEN YOU BEGIN...
   THERE IS NO JUDGMENT ABOUT THIS!
BE FIERCE ABOUT GETTING THIS TIME & SPACE,
   BUT DON'T BE HARD ON YOURSELF IF YOU FEEL
   YOU ARE NOT DOING IT RIGHT OR WELL ENOUGH.
   BE COMPASSIONATE TOWARD YOURSELF.
   BUT DON'T BE AFRAID TO CHALLENGE YOURSELF EITHER.
   LET YOURSELF BE LED BY THE SPIRIT.

ALSO, DON'T MAKE JUDGMENTS ABOUT *WHAT COMES* TO YOU
   IN THIS DAILY MEETING.
   IT IS WHAT IT IS.

IF WE ARE DRAWN **TO THE PAST AND DIFFICULT TIMES**,
   THEN WE MIGHT FACE FAILURE
   OR WHERE OTHERS FAILED US. (SEE LORD'S PRAYER)
   WE'VE BEEN CARRYING IT AROUND,
   AND NOW WE'RE NOTICING IT.
   LOOK AT THAT.
   IF IT'S OLD ANGER OR RESENTMENT,
      DECIDE IF YOU WANT
      TO BEAR IT ANY LONGER.

JESUS SAID, *"WHEN YOU STAND IN PRAYER,*
      *FORGIVE **WHATEVER** YOU HAVE*
      *AGAINST **ANYONE**."*
                                    MARK 11:25

JESUS LIKED TRAVELING LIGHT...
   MORE ROOM ON THE HARD DRIVE FOR NEW THINGS...
   LESS EMOTIONAL SPAM.

IF YOU FEEL **GRIEF** WELLING UP OVER THE
   LOSS OF A LOVED ONE, THEN GOOD.
   IT'S TIME TO GRIEVE...
   AND BE DRAWN INTO THE DEPTHS OF LOVING.
   THAT WILL TAKE YOU INTO YOUR SOUL LIKE NOTHING ELSE
   AND OPEN YOUR HEART TO A TENDERNESS
   YOU MAY HAVE NOT FELT FOR YEARS.

IF IN YOUR ALONENESS YOU FIND YOURSELF **ANXIOUS**
   ABOUT THE FUTURE, YOU ARE DEFINITELY ONE OF US.
   WE DO HAVE A LOT OF FEARS.
   LET'S NOT PRETEND LIKE SIMON PETER
            THAT WE ARE FEARLESS.

WE'RE AFRAID. SO WE COME WITH THAT.
    MAYBE WE WILL HEAR THAT VOICE
            THAT KEEPS SAYING TO US,

"COURAGE! IT'S ME! DON'T BE AFRAID".   MARK 6:50

    AND IN OUR ALONENESS, WE CAN CRY OUT
    AND FIND OURSELVES MYSTERIOUSLY "HELD".

SO WHATEVER HAPPENS IS
    WHAT IS SUPPOSED TO HAPPEN
    AND IT WILL TAKE US SOMEWHERE, AND
    WE WILL BE ON A JOURNEY, THE ULTIMATE ADVENTURE.

OUR ANCESTORS FEARED THE DESERTS IN THEIR LIVES,
    BUT FOUND THAT SOMETHING HAPPENED DEEP IN THEIR
    INNER BEING THAT WAS PRECIOUS AND DEFINING...

ON THAT SILENT RETREAT IN 1978, THE SCRIPTURE THAT CAME
TO ME WITH FRESH MEANING WERE THE WORDS THAT GOD
SPOKE TO THE ANCESTORS IN THE DESERT:

"BUT LOOK,
    I AM GOING TO SEDUCE YOU (ISRAEL),
    AND LEAD YOU
        INTO THE DESERT,
            AND THERE
                I WILL SPEAK
                    TO YOUR HEART"

                                    HOSEA 2:16

THE 2ND PRACTICE: IMMERSION IN THE BELOVED

THE 2ND PRACTICE NESTS INSIDE THE 1ST PRACTICE.
  IT BECOMES A WAY OF BEING IN SOLITUDE,
  A DEEP POSSIBILITY FOR THE DAILY MEETING.
  IT BUILDS UPON OUR INTENTION TO BE WITH OUR SOUL
  AND WITH GOD.
I SEE THIS THROUGH THESE **4 LENSES**:

A) *"THE SPIRIT OF GOD HAS COME UPON ME."*

IN THE HEBREW BIBLE THE PROPHET ISAIAH
GIVES VOICE TO THE DIVINE:

"HERE IS MY SERVANT WHOM I UPHOLD.
MY CHOSEN ONE IN WHOM MY SOUL DELIGHTS.
I HAVE SENT MY SPIRIT UPON HIM/HER."
                    ISAIAH 42:1 (1ST SERVANT SONG)

THE SERVANT IN THESE 4 SERVANT SONGS
  (IS. 42, 49, 50, 52-53) CAN BE ISRAEL, OR AN INDIVIDUAL,
  OR YOU... WONDERFULLY AMBIGUOUS.
SO IT IS NOT SURPRISING THAT JESUS IN HIS
  RENEWING RITUAL IN THE JORDAN RIVER WITH
  "WILD" JOHN HEARS SIMILAR ANCIENT WORDS:
      "THE HEAVENS WERE TORN APART
      AND THE SPIRIT DESCENDED...
      'YOU ARE MY SON, THE BELOVED
      IN WHOM MY SOUL TAKES DELIGHT.'"   MARK 1:11

THIS IS A SEMINAL MOMENT IN JESUS' LIFE,
  FOR HE ENTERS INTO THE GENEALOGY OF THOSE
  WHO HAVE STEPPED INTO THIS SACRED SPACE.
  THOSE WHO LONG FOR GOD COME HERE.
  THOSE WHO CRY OUT FOR THE SPIRIT OF GOD ARE HEARD.
  THOSE WHO HAVE TRIED OTHER PATHS
      AND EXHAUST THEMSELVES COME HERE.
SOMETHING CONVENTIONAL CRACKS AND A CRY GOES OUT.
SOMETHING TRADITIONAL IMPLODES AND THIS PRAYER CRY IS HEARD:
    "COME, SPIRIT OF GOD. COME!
      WHAT I AM TO BE CANNOT BE... WITHOUT YOU!
      COME SPIRIT... COME SPIRIT! COME!!!!"

THE POET RAINER MARIA RILKE FEELS ENCASED INSIDE SOLID
ROCK AND CAN'T FIND HIS WAY OUT. HE WRITES:
   "*YOU BE THE MASTER! MAKE YOURSELF FIERCE, BREAK IN:*
    THEN YOUR GREAT TRANSFORMING WILL HAPPEN TO ME,
    AND MY GREAT GRIEF CRY WILL HAPPEN TO YOU."   [7]

AND SO JESUS HAD LEFT HIS MOTHER,
     LEFT HIS RESPONSIBILITY AS THE ELDEST SON,
     LEFT HIS HOME AND HIS SYNAGOGUE,
     LEFT HIS FAMILY AND FRIENDS, LEFT HIS JOB,
     AND CAME TO A WILD MENTOR-MAN
         IN A COLD, WILD RIVER.
THIS WAS NOT ONE OF THE TAMED PRIESTS OF
     THE TEMPLE IN JERUSALEM.
THIS WAS NOT THE CALM WATERS OF
     THE CLEANSING CISTERNS AT THE TEMPLE.
THIS WAS NOT THE PREDICTABLE COURSE IN RELIGIOUS STUDIES.
THIS WAS AN UNTAMED MAN IN A WILD RIVER
     WITH A SOUL-STIRRING CEREMONY.
AND THE *UNTAMED DIVINE* CAME TO JESUS ...
         AND HE BECAME A SPIRIT-PERSON.

IS IT TIME FOR US TO ENTER THIS SAME SACRED SPACE...?

IS IT TIME FOR US TO CRY OUT FOR THE SPIRIT OF GOD?
     "COME SPIRIT OF GOD...
      COME SPIRIT... COME!"

THIS CRY IS **ALWAYS** HEARD.
  THE SPIRIT AWAITS AN OPPORTUNITY,
   AN OPENING TO
      COME <u>NEAR</u>...
         EVEN <u>**UPON**</u> US.

WHEN OUR DESIRE BECOMES STRONG ENOUGH....
     SOMETHING SHATTERS IN US
        & THE SPIRIT COMES....
        IN AN UNPREDICTABLE, UNIQUE WAY....
        OFTEN SUBTLE.... UNEXPECTED...
        UNEXPLAINABLE...DREAM-LIKE...

WE REALIZE WE ARE REALLY *<u>NOT ALONE</u>*...

     AND THERE IS SOME KIND OF *<u>DESTINY</u>* AHEAD...

B) "I AM BELOVED"

> "YOU ARE MY SON/DAUGHTER, THE BELOVED
> IN WHOM MY SOUL TAKES DELIGHT".
> > (VOICE TO JESUS AT RIVER)

IT'S CLEAR THAT JESUS HEARD THESE WORDS...
   THAT GOD CALLED HIM "BELOVED".
HE CERTAINLY STRUGGLES IN THE DESERT WITH QUESTIONS
   ABOUT WHETHER THAT WAS REALLY "GOD" SPEAKING
   AND WHAT THAT MEANT.

DID IT MEAN HE WOULD NOT BE *LIKE* OTHER PEOPLE?
DID IT MEAN HE WOULD BE *PROTECTED* FROM ANY HARM?
   (SEE MT. 4:6)
DID IT MEAN HE WAS THE *ONLY* BELOVED?
OR DID HE HEAR SUCH WORDS OF DIVINE TENDERNESS,
   THAT *IT BECAME HIS MESSAGE...* HIS GOOD NEWS?

AND HAD GOD BECOME *MORE* THAN AN ANCIENT,
   SACRED WORD?
   HAD GOD BECOME AN ENERGY SO PRESENT THAT IT BECAME THE
   EVIDENCE FOR HIS BOLD STATEMENTS:

> "THE REIGN OF GOD IS AT HAND...
>   AROUND YOU... WITHIN YOU."

AFTER 42 YEARS OF STUDYING/PROCESSING THIS,
I BELIEVE UNAMBIGUOUSLY THAT JESUS EMBRACED
   "I AM BELOVED"
      AS THE LYNCH-PIN FOR HIS LIFE.

AND THAT HIS GROWING LOVE FOR GOD
BROUGHT GOD FROM BEING:

> *"ADONAI"* ("LORD": HEBREW SUBSTITUTE
>   FOR UNNAMABLE ONE), OR
> *"ALAHA"* ("ONENESS": ARAMAIC WORD FOR GOD),
>   TO ALSO BEING
> *"ABBA"* (ARAMAIC TERM OF FAMILIAL ENDEARMENT)

"ABBA" BECOMES FOR JESUS A TENDER,
   INTIMATE NAME FOR "THE DIVINE BELOVED".
AND IMPORTANTLY, AS JESUS OWNS BEING "BELOVED",
   GOD BECOMES "BELOVED" TO HIM.

DON'T MISS THIS.
THIS IS AN EVOLUTION IN JESUS' SELF-IMAGE WHICH ALSO
    BECOMES AN EVOLUTION IN THE PERCEPTION
    OF THE CREATOR.
        THIS IS A FALLING IN LOVE.

THERE IS A BANK ON THE SIDE OF THIS RIVER,
    AND A "FALLING" HERE INTO THIS RIVER,
        AND AN EMBRACE IN THIS RIVER....

I ALSO BELIEVE THAT THIS WAS ALL PART OF THE
    "GOOD NEWS" OF JESUS.
AND THAT JESUS' MESSAGE ABOUT GOD WAS THAT
    GOD WAS THE **TENDER PARENT** IN THE PARABLE
    OF THE "LOST SON(S)" (LUKE 15),
    AND THAT GOD WAS THE **SHEPHERD**
        LOOKING FOR THE "LOST SHEEP",
    AND THAT ***GOD WAS THE BELOVED***.

AND THAT NO MATTER
    HOW YOU HAVE BEEN DEMEANED, REJECTED, ABUSED,
    THAT ***YOU ARE BELOVED TOO***...

YOU ARE GOD'S BELOVED CHILD!
AND EVEN IGNORING THAT DOESN'T CHANGE IT.

WE ARE THE BELOVED AS THE IMAGE OF THE CREATOR
    WHO IS UNVEILED AS THE BELOVED.
    JESUS SAW BEHIND THE CURTAIN IN THE TEMPLE,
    THE "BURKA" OF GOD, AND SAW THE **BELOVED**.

THIS, OF COURSE, FLIES IN THE FACE OF A LOT
    WE HAVE BEEN TAUGHT OR EXPERIENCED IN OUR LIFE.
    WHO ELSE FEELS THAT WE ARE BELOVED?
    IF YOU HAVE PEOPLE LIKE THAT IN YOUR LIFE,
        YOU HAVE BEEN BLESSED!
    BUT MOST PEOPLE HAVE NOT EXPERIENCED
        MUCH OF THIS,
        AND WHEN THEY DO,
        MAY GO TO THE ENDS OF THE EARTH
        TO STAY NEAR IT.
    IT IS SO LUMINOUS WHEN IT IS REAL ,
        AND SOMETIMES, EVEN WHEN IT IS NOT.
    EVEN THE **ILLUSION** OF IT IS POWERFUL.
    CHECK OUT POPULAR MUSIC ON THE SUBJECT.

SO WHEREVER YOU HAVE BEEN AND HOW YOU HAVE BEEN
        HURT / DISAPPOINTED BY RELATIONSHIPS...
ARE YOU READY TO ***DARE TO BELIEVE***
        THAT YOU ARE A BELOVED OF GOD?

AND THEN, BEGIN TO ***TRUST*** THAT?
AND LET IT ***SHAPE YOUR BEING
        & YOUR JOURNEY?***

ON RETREATS WE WOULD SOMETIMES GO AROUND "BEHOLDING"
EACH PERSON WITH ACCEPTING "SOFT EYES". LOOKING DEEPLY
INTO EACH, WE WOULD SAY TO THEM:
   "YOU ARE A BELOVED CHILD OF GOD"
    AND LET IT SINK IN... AND IN.

A MANTRA/ MEDITATION FOR THE 2ND PRACTICE COULD
BE REMINDING OURSELVES BY SAYING:

"I am Beloved"

"I am your Beloved son/daughter."

C) "I ONCE WAS LOST, BUT NOW I AM FOUND"

*"WHAT WOMAN WITH TEN GOLD COINS WOULD NOT, IF SHE LOST ONE,
LIGHT A LAMP AND SWEEP OUT THE HOUSE AND SEARCH THOROUGHLY
TILL SHE FOUND IT? AND THEN WHEN SHE HAD FOUND IT,
 CALL TOGETHER HER FRIENDS AND NEIGHBORS, SAYING,
'REJOICE WITH ME, I HAVE FOUND THE GOLD COIN I LOST.'
IN THE SAME WAY, I TELL YOU, THERE IS REJOICING
AMONG THE ANGELS OF GOD
OVER ONE RECOVERED LOST PERSON."*   *LUKE 15:8F.*

I HAVE AGONIZED WITH THE PARENTS OF THE HIGH SCHOOL
    SENIOR WHO DISAPPEARED ON A GRADUATION TRIP TO
    ARUBA. THOUGH THEY WERE DIVORCED,
    THEY BOTH WENT TO ARUBA AND BEGAN THEIR OWN
    SEARCH. FRUSTRATED WITH LOCAL AUTHORITIES,
    THEY HIRED SOMEONE WHO FINDS THE LOST.
    THEY DUG IN THE GROUND, INTERVIEWED EVERYONE
     AND FINALLY BEGAN TO COMB THE SEA
     LOOKING FOR A FISHING CRATE ON THE BOTTOM.

THEY PUT EVERYTHING, I MEAN EVERYTHING ASIDE,
    AND WITH NO THOUGHT OF COST, DEVOTED THEIR LIVES TO
    FINDING THEIR BELOVED LOST DAUGHTER.
IT WAS OVER 2 YEARS, AND THEY WERE STILL LOOKING...
    NOW EVEN FOR HER LIFELESS BODY.

WHEN WE ARE LOST, IS *THIS* WHAT IS GOING ON?
DOES THE DIVINE BELOVED <u>FOCUS</u> ON ME,
    AND <u>SEARCH</u> DILIGENTLY, THOROUGHLY,
    WITH ABANDON AND BROKEN-HEARTED DEVOTION...
    UNTIL I AM RECOVERED?

*"It is 1964. After being an atheist for 5 years, I am
    running down a lonely winter road in Ames, Iowa.
    I begin to see crosses ahead of me and behind me,
    no matter how far I run.
    Then I begin to hear a voice & feel a presence
    no matter how fast I run.
    And I can't find a place to hide any longer
    from One who is determined to break through
    my cynicism & anger to my lonely soul.
    I have been grasped so lovingly,
    I can no longer resist.
    I don't have any idea what to do with this,
    but I have crossed a river (or entered one).
    It doesn't matter that the next morning
    the crosses are mere telephone poles again.
    I am never the same."*

<u>THIS IS A LOT TO TAKE IN</u>. TAKE A BIG BREATH...
    WE'RE SAYING THAT THE CREATOR OF THE UNIVERSE IS
        ... <u>THAT</u> INTERESTED IN US....
        ... <u>THAT</u> WE ARE VALUABLE TO THE DIVINE DRAMA
            AFOOT
        ... <u>THAT</u> THERE IS A TRAGIC INCOMPLETENESS,
            A HOLE IN THE UNIVERSE'S DESTINY WITHOUT US
        ... <u>THAT</u> WHEN WE ARE RECOVERED,
            THERE IS A CELESTIAL CELEBRATION

<u>THAT'S A STRETCH</u> FOR MOST OF US.
<u>BUT THAT IS WHAT THE WHOLE THING IS ABOUT!</u>
<u>THIS</u> IS THE GOOD NEWS.
SO IF YOU ARE RUNNING,
    STOP AND LOOK OVER YOUR SHOULDER
    AND AHEAD OF YOU.

YOU ARE NOT ALONE OUT THERE.
    AND IF YOU HAVE STOPPED RUNNING,
    JOIN IN THE GREAT CELEBRATION.
    BELIEVE IT OR NOT, IT'S FOR **YOU**!

D) *"A TEMPLE OF GOD AM I"*

" YHVH SPOKE TO MOSES, SAYING...
'HAVE THEM MAKE ME A HOLY PLACE ,
AND I WILL DWELL IN THEIR MIDST."   EXODUS 25: 1F.

IN THE HEBREW BIBLE, THE PEOPLE ARE INSTRUCTED TO
    BUILD A **"MISHKAN"** (HEBREW: MISH — KAWN').
    IN ENGLISH IT WAS A DWELLING PLACE OR TABERNACLE.
    THE ARK OF THE COVENANT WAS ACADIA WOOD OVERLAID
    WITH PURE GOLD INSIDE AND OUT. AROUND THE ARK WAS
    WOVEN THE TABERNACLE FROM FINE-TWISTED LINEN IN
    BLUE & PURPLE & CRIMSON YARN.   THE CARVERS &
    GOLDSMITHS & WEAVERS MADE A ***PHYSICAL*** TABERNACLE
    IN WHICH THE PRESENCE OF THE HOLY ONE WOULD DWELL,
    EVENTUALLY BECOMING THE TEMPLE IN JERUSALEM.
    DURING THE EXILE OF THE HEBREW PEOPLE, THE PEOPLE
    WERE IN A FOREIGN LAND, WITH A FOREIGN LANGUAGE,
    AND **NO TEMPLE**.

EZEKIEL HAD TO POINT OUT THAT THE PRESENCE OF "YHVH"
    COULD NOT BE LIMITED TO THE PHYSICAL TEMPLE.

  AND THE <u>MYSTICAL TRADITION TAUGHT THAT EACH OF US</u>
    <u>WAS ALSO TO BUILD A DWELLING PLACE/ TEMPLE</u>
    <u>(MISHKAN) IN OUR OWN HEARTS.</u>
    THIS COULD NOT BE DESTROYED BY ARMIES OR EMPIRES.
    "YHVY" WAS ALWAYS THE "MISHKAN" IN WHICH WE CAN
    DWELL IN SECRET SAFETY.
    "MISHKAN" IS A DWELLING PLACE FOR THE DIVINE
    PRESENCE:

"O LORD, YOU HAVE BEEN OUR REFUGE (MISHKAN)
* FROM AGE TO AGE"*   PSALM 90:1

"YOU WHO LIVE IN THE SECRET PLACE OF
* ELYON (THE MOST HIGH)...*
* SAYING TO "YHVH" (THE NAMELESS ONE),*
* MY REFUGE (MISHKAN), MY FORTRESS,*
* MY GOD IN WHOM I TRUST."*   PSALM 91:1F.

*"IN THE SECRET OF GOD'S TABERNACLE (MISHKAN) SHALL
GOD HIDE ME"*   PSALM 27:5

WHEN THE PHYSICAL TEMPLE (MISHKAN) WAS <u>DESTROYED</u>
   BY THE ROMANS IN 70 C.E., IT WAS DEVASTATING
   AND ALL THE MORE URGENT FOR ONE TO BUILD
   ONE'S OWN "MISHKAN".

   <u>**SO YOUR LIFE'S WORK WAS TO BUILD
   A PLACE INSIDE YOURSELF FOR THE HOLY ONE TO DWELL.**</u>

THIS IS BUILDING AN INFRASTRUCTURE FOR THE SPIRIT.
<u>**NOW**</u> MYSTICAL SPIRITUALITY BECAME VITAL,
   EVEN ESSENTIAL.
   WITHOUT THIS INNER "MISHKAN",
    PEOPLE WOULD LIVE WITH A VAST EMPTINESS INSIDE,
   AND LOSE THE SACREDNESS OF THEIR BEING,
    LIKE A GREAT CATHEDRAL
        WITH NO ART, NO MUSIC,
        NO AWE, NO PRESENCE, NO LIFE.

OR THERE IS ALWAYS THE DANGER OF TURNING THE
   SCRIPTURES, OR THE CLERGY, OR ANYONE OUT THERE
   INTO THE "MISHKAN" AND RELIGIOUSLY
   FALLING INTO IDOLATRY.
   LET'S JUST SAY THAT THIS IS EXTREMELY EASY TO DO.

WE HAVE JESUS IN JOHN 14:23...

   *"ANYONE WHO LOVES ME WILL KEEP MY WORD
     AND ABBA WILL LOVE THEM
     AND WE SHALL COME TO THEM
     AND MAKE A DWELLING PLACE (MISHKAN)
    IN THEM."*

AND THEN PAUL WRITING TO THE CHURCH IN CORINTH:

   *"DO YOU NOT REALIZE THAT YOU ARE
        A TEMPLE (MISHKAN) OF GOD
        WITH THE SPIRIT OF GOD
        LIVING IN YOU?"*   I COR.3:16

SO THE GREAT CHALLENGE OF THE SPIRITUAL JOURNEY
    IS TO <u>BUILD THIS "MISHKAN" FOR THE BELOVED</u> INSIDE.

THEN OUR <u>BODIES BECOME SACRED</u> AGAIN.

AND OUR VERY SELVES BECOME A <u>HOUSE OF BELONGING</u>.

AND WE <u>EMBODY THE HOLY ONE</u>.

AND WE ARE <u>ROOTED IN THE ETERNAL</u>,

THIS BRINGS US <u>COURAGE,</u>
                   <u>COMPASSION,</u>
                       <u>AND A DEEP PEACE</u>.

THE POET KABIR SEES THIS AS A SMALL RUBY THAT EVERYONE
WANTS AND SEARCHES FOR. HE SAYS:

"KABIR'S INSTINCT TOLD HIM IT WAS INSIDE,
AND WHAT IT WAS WORTH,
AND HE WRAPPED IT UP CAREFULLY
IN HIS HEART CLOTH."   [8]

HERE IS A <u>BREATHING PRAYER</u> FOR THE 2ND PRACTICE,
THAT CAN ALSO BE A CHANT:

Breathe in: *The Spirit of God has come upon me*

"   out: *I am Beloved*

"   in: *I once was lost, but now am found*

"   out: *A temple of God am I*

THE METAPHOR OF THE 2ND PRACTICE:
"THE RIVER"

"It is April 2009. I am soon to retire, leaving a church I love for a new calling. I am disoriented & grieving.
I dream:

> *"I'm in Kenya, I think, but I don't know where.*
> *It is very different and beautiful. I go down to the*
> *river that flows through this land. It is clear & stunning*
> *and everyone is coming together along the river.*
> *I'm a little anxious about not knowing where I am".*

I get it. My retirement will bring me to a place new & foreign to me , but there will be community and that amazing river of God that flows through us all.

THE **"RIVER"** IS AN IMPORTANT IMAGE & METAPHOR HERE.
   JESUS WENT INTO THE "RIVER OF GOD".
   HE HAD STUDIED THE RIVER,
   AND STORIES OF OTHERS WHO HAD GONE INTO THE RIVER.
   BUT HE WENT TO JOHN WHO HAD
   ACTUALLY GONE INTO THE RIVER...
   AND JOHN HAD AN ACTUAL "LITERAL" RIVER TOO,
   THE JORDAN.

NOW YOU COULD GO INTO THE "LITERAL RIVER",
          AND **NOT** GO INTO THE "RIVER OF GOD".

YOU HAD TO HAVE A WILD PASSION FOR GOD
   TO GO INTO THIS **"RIVER"**.
   YOU HAD TO TRY OUT A FEW **OTHER** THINGS...
   AND KNOW THAT YOU COULD **NOT** LIVE
   WITHOUT GOING INTO THE "RIVER OF GOD"

YOU HAD TO GO INTO RELIGION AND ITS TRADITIONS
   AND COME UP **DRY**..
YOU HAD TO GO INTO SPIRITUALITY &
   STILL FEEL THAT **HUNGRY DESIRE**,
   TO WANT TO DIVE INTO **THIS** "RIVER".

SO WHEN JESUS SAYS, **"FOLLOW ME"**,

      A LOT OF PEOPLE WANT TO COME,
      BUT WE MAY FIND OURSELVES IN THAT CROWD,
      STANDING ON THE BANK OF THAT RIVER.

AND WHEN JESUS GOES IN
        AND CALLS TO US,

"COME INTO THE RIVER OF GOD",

WE MAY STAY THERE ON THE BANK
        A LONG........ LONG TIME...

IS THIS WHERE WE HAVE COME NOW?...
    IF WE WOULD **ENTER** THE SPIRITUALITY OF JESUS,
    NO LONGER JUST **STUDY**...
    IF WE WOULD COME INTO THE
        MOVEMENT OF GOD'S SPIRIT...

    IF WE WOULD LET OURSELVES
        BE **IMMERSED IN THIS ONE**...
    IF WE WOULD **FALL** INTO THE BELOVED'S EMBRACE...
        THEN WE WILL WANT TO GO **INTO THIS RIVER**.
    NO! DON'T BE A LITERALIST & GET BAPTIZED AGAIN!

GO INTO THE "RIVER OF GOD":

Close your eyes,
    stand on the bank,

    breathe deeply,

    as you breathe out,

drop away your hesitation & shame,

pray with unequivocal desire,

and when you are ready......

        dive into the River,

        fall into the Divine's longing embrace,

        immerse yourself in the Beloved's presence....

IN THE RIVER WE BEGIN TO KNOW,
    AS EXPERIENCE, THE WAY OF JESUS.

THIS IS WHERE THE SPIRITUALITY OF JESUS LEADS US.

REFLECTIONS ON "ABBA & I ARE ONE"

WHEN JESUS SAYS, *"ABBA & I ARE ONE"* (JOHN 10:30),
   IT HAS OFTEN BEEN TAKEN TO DEFINE
   THE ABSOLUTELY UNIQUE CHARACTER OF JESUS.
   THERE WAS A LAW AGAINST THIS "BLASPHEMY",
   AND THIS SET HIM AGAINST HIS OWN "RELIGIOUS TRADITION".

   "YOU ARE ONLY A MAN, YET CLAIM TO BE GOD".
   AND THEY PREPARED TO STONE HIM.

   JESUS IN JOHN 10 ARGUES THAT
   WE ARE **ALL** "**SONS OF GOD**",
   IF THE WORD OF GOD IS ADDRESSING US.
   AND IF HIS CRITICS WOULD, THEY COULD SEE THAT
   HIS WORKS REVEAL THAT
   "ABBA IS IN ME, AND I AM IN ABBA".   (JOHN 10:38)

THIS MAKES NO SENSE TO THE
   STANDARD RELIGIOUS TRADITIONS.
   BUT IN THE **MYSTICAL TRADITION OF JUDIASM**
   (AND OTHER MYSTICAL TRADITIONS), IT MAKES A LOT OF SENSE.
JESUS IS TEACHING HERE FROM THE **RIVER**, NOT THE DRY BANK.
   AND OTHERS HAVE BEEN THERE AS WELL.

THOMAS AQUINAS SAID THAT JESUS INTENDED TO MAKE US
"PARTAKERS OF DIVINE NATURE". [9]

AND FROM INDIA, TAGORE, THE POET AND SPIRITUAL GUIDE OF GHANDI,
SAYS THAT THE LORD HAS TAKEN HIM AS A PARTNER IN ALL THIS
WEALTH. FOR YOU, LORD, HAVE...
   "DECKED THYSELF IN BEAUTY TO CAPTIVATE MY HEART.
   AND FOR THIS THY LOVE LOSES ITSELF IN THE LOVE OF THY LOVER,
   AND THERE ART THOU SEEN IN THE PERFECT UNION OF TWO." [10]

IT IS **_ALWAYS_** MIS-UNDERSTOOD.
   IT COMES OFF AS ARROGANCE, INFLATION, HERESY,
   DELUSION, PSYCHOSIS.... NOTHING GOOD HERE.

AND **JESUS ENCOUNTERS ALL OF THAT**,
   AS WELL AS JEALOUSY, ENVY, AND HOSTILITY.
SOME SAY HE WAS KILLED BECAUSE OF THAT...
   OTHERS HAVE TOO.

IT IS SUCH A DANGEROUS STATEMENT.
     WE DON'T WANT TO ENCOURAGE THIS.
     SO IT HAS TO BE A SINGULAR STATEMENT
     BY THE **ONLY** SON OF GOD.
     NO ONE ELSE DARE PRESUME
     SUCH A RELATIONSHIP WITH GOD.

BUT WHAT IF YOU'RE IN THE RIVER OF GOD,
     AND YOU BECOME **ONE**
     WITH THE RIVER, IF ONLY FOR A TIME?
     WHAT IF LANGUAGE CAN'T
     EXPRESS HOW YOU FEEL **ANY OTHER WAY**?

DO WE NOT SAY THAT MARRIAGE IS WHEN
     TWO SHALL BECOME **ONE**?
     IS THAT WHAT IT MEANS TO **"FALL IN LOVE"**...
     TO OVERCOME THE SEPARATION
        THAT WE CONTINUALLY LIVE IN,
     AND FEEL AT **ONE** WITH SOMEONE ELSE?

CAN WE NOT FALL IN LOVE WITH THE DIVINE BELOVED,
     AND BE IN THE RIVER OF GOD FOR A TIME,
     AND COME OUT DRIPPING WET AND SAY,
        "ABBA & I ARE ONE"?

AND WHEN JESUS SAYS, **"FOLLOW ME"**,
     HE REALLY MEANS ***ALL THE WAY,***
     THE WHOLE JOURNEY, ALL YOUR LIFE,
     INTO THE RIVER,
     INTO YOUR DYING, AND
     INTO THE JOURNEY BEYOND THIS LIFE.

I KNOW WE HAVE BEEN WARNED ABOUT THIS.
I KNOW THIS CANNOT BE
     TAKEN LIGHTLY.

BUT IF THAT IS WHERE JESUS IS TAKING US,

     THEN THAT'S WHERE I WANT TO GO TOO....

"i in you

you in me

safe & warm

in thee"

THE 3RD PRACTICE: OWNING MY DARKNESS

"It is Oct. 2009. I am retired and uncertain about the next steps in my new career. I dream:
> *'I come home and the house is dark and door ajar.*
> *I've been gone for days. An intruder appears, but*
> *doesn't threaten me. I grab a big pole as a weapon and*
> *begin to attack him. I can only attack gently. He doesn't*
> *defend himself. I realize he is not an enemy and decide*
> *to let him stay. I introduce myself. His name is Jim.*
> *(Hey, that's my name) He seems like a nice guy, has a*
> *certain strength, is wily, but not malicious.*
> *We have a new houseguest.'*

I wake up wondering who is this "shadow" of mine that appears to be a strange intruder, but actually is a part of me that I don't know ? I think I need this "Jim" now... his strength, wilyness, and presence. I need all the help that is in me now. I'm glad he is moving in."

IF THE 1ST PRACTICE GIVES US ***SPACE*** ....
      TO HAVE A MEETING WITH GOD & OUR OWN SOUL,
      AND THE 2ND PRACTICE BRINGS US
         AN ***IMMERSION*** ....IN ***GRACE***
      THAT CAN SOAK INTO OUR BRAIN & OUR BONES,
      AND SHIFT OUR COMFORT LEVEL IN OUR OWN SKIN,
THEN THE 2ND PRACTICE CAN GIVE US THE
      STABILITY & COURAGE TO ***FACE....*** OUR DARKNESS.

THE 3RD PRACTICE CAN BE DIFFICULT ENOUGH
      EVEN WITH THAT SAFETY NET.
      BUT WITHOUT THAT HEALING OF THE SELF,
      WE DON'T HAVE THE SPIRITUAL INFRASTRUCTURE
      TO ***ADMIT*** OUR DARKNESS, LET ALONE ***DEAL*** WITH IT.
      WE FEEL WE HAVE TO REMAIN IN **DENIAL**.

IN THE INTRODUCTION TO THE INWARD JOURNEY (PART 1/2),
      WE SAW HOW THE **DARKNESS/SHADOW** INVOLVES
        THE **EGO-CENTRIC EGO,**
           OUR WOUNDS,
           AND THE DIVINE IMAGE.
HERE WE SEE HOW THEY **INTER-RELATE**
      IN JESUS' SPIRITUALITY.

"THEY WENT AND WERE BAPTIZED BY JOHN IN THE JORDAN RIVER
'OWNING THEIR SINS'"   MARK 1:5

JOHN'S CEREMONY FOCUSED ON PEOPLE
    OWNING THEIR DARKNESS,
     AND THEIR **LONGING TO LIVE** A NEW LIFE.
     JESUS PARTICIPATED IN THIS CEREMONY
     AND IT WAS *TRANSFORMING* FOR HIM.
JESUS FELT THE SPIRIT OF GOD DESCEND
     AND A NEW INTIMACY WITH GOD.
     HE HEARD LUMINOUS WORDS OF LOVE & DESTINY.
    AFTER THAT, THERE WAS A CLOSE CONNECTION FOR JESUS
     <u>**BETWEEN OWNING OUR DARKNESS**</u>
     <u>**AND INTIMACY WITH THE DIVINE BELOVED**</u>!
     THIS IS CRUCIAL. READ THAT AGAIN!

JESUS GOES INTO THE DESERT TO STRUGGLE
     WITH THE OBSTACLES TO HIS DESTINY,
     ESPECIALLY THE EVER EAGER **EGO**:
        THE DESIRE FOR RECOGNITION AND FOR POWER.
AFTER HE STRUGGLED, IT IS TOLD THAT HE WAS
     WITH THE WILD ANIMALS,
     AND THE ANGELS LOOKED AFTER HIM.   (MARK 1:13)
     BOTH ARE SIGNS OF THE BELOVED'S PRESENCE & CARE.

YOU COULD AGAIN SAY THAT THERE IS A CONNECTION
     BETWEEN AN EXPERIENCE OF GOD'S *GRACE*
        (GOING INTO THE <u>**RIVER OF GOD**</u>)
     AND THE DESIRE TO *FACE* INWARD IMPEDIMENTS
        (GOING INTO THE <u>**DESERT OF GOD**</u>).

THERE IS ALSO A <u>**CONNECTION**</u> BETWEEN OUR
     INNER DARKNESS AND OUR HEALING PROCESS.

JESUS ASKS THE SICK MAN SITTING BY THE HEALING POOL
     FOR YEARS: *<u>"DO YOU WANT TO BE WELL AGAIN?"</u>*
          (JOHN 5:6)

JESUS IS ASKING THE MAN TO GET A HOLD ON HIS
     DARKER MOTIVES, BEFORE HE CHALLENGES
     THE HEALING POWER OF THE POOL.

BUT WE WILL FOCUS ON JESUS' PREMIER TEACHING IN MATTHEW 7:2F.

"WHY DO YOU OBSERVE THE SPLINTER IN YOUR BROTHER/SISTER'S EYE
AND NEVER NOTICE
THE LOG IN YOUR OWN?
TAKE THE LOG OUT OF YOUR OWN EYE FIRST,
AND THEN YOU WILL SEE CLEARLY ENOUGH TO TAKE
THE SPLINTER OUT OF YOUR BROTHER/SISTER'S EYE."

THIS IS HOW IT WORKS:
I AM REALLY ANNOYED...
I MEAN **I AM UPSET** WITH MY WIFE
AND I SAY: "YOU ARE ALWAYS SO CRITICAL...
              YOU HAVE THIS ATTITUDE...
              WHY ARE YOU ALWAYS SO ANGRY....?"
I'M GETTING MYSELF WORKED INTO A REAL LATHER HERE.......
I'M ON A ROLL NOW....
              "IF YOU CARED AT ALL YOU WOULD...
              YOU NEED TO GET YOURSELF TOGETHER...
              I KNOW A COUNSELOR FOR YOU..."

THERE **NOW** I FEEL BETTER,
IT'S NOT GOOD TO CARRY THIS AROUND...
              OR DO I FEEL **WORSE**...?
YOU HAVE TO ADMIT IT WAS A **BOLD DEFENSE**!
THE BEST DEFENSE IS ALWAYS A GOOD OFFENSE, ISN'T IT?
A RETAILATORY STRIKE!
SHE WAS ATTACKING ME AFTER ALL...... WASN'T SHE!

SO WHAT IS GOING ON HERE...

I AM CRITICIZING HER FOR **HER ATTITUDE** (SPLINTER)
     WITHOUT BEING ABLE TO LOOK AT **MY OWN** ATTITUDE,
     DEFENSIVENESS, ANGER (LOG).

LET'S FACE IT,
     IT'S MUCH EASIER TO GO AFTER HER "FLAW"
     THAN TO GO AFTER MY "NEUROSIS".

JESUS' IMAGE TEACHES US:

1) **I HAVE TO BEGIN WITH MYSELF.**
   I HAVE TO TAKE MY OWN LOG & LEARN WHAT IT IS!
   I HAVE TO BE ABLE TO LOOK AT MY ATTITUDE,
   MY EMOTIONAL STATE.
   THIS WOULD REQUIRE ME TO HAVE SOME
   SEMBLANCE OF A 1ST PRACTICE.
   I NEED SOME **SPACE** ....
   TO REFLECT ON WHERE I AM "COMING FROM".

2) **I HAVE TO OWN IT.**
   IT IS MY LOG, MY PERSONAL, MY VERY OWN MISSILE
   DEFENSE SYSTEM. I DEVELOPED IT, PUT IT INTO ACTION,
   AND IT BEARS MY OWN UNIQUE COPYWRITED FOOTPRINT.
   I'M GOOD AT IT AND I THINK I DESERVE SOME
   RECOGNITION HERE.
   IT IS VERY, VERY HARD TO BE ABLE TO
   LOOK AT THIS AND OWN IT,
   UNLESS I HAVE REALIZED THAT
   I AM MORE THAN THIS,
   AND THAT I AM ACCEPTED,
   EVEN **BELOVED**... INCLUDING THIS.
   THIS IS THE IMPORTANCE OF THE 2ND PRACTICE AGAIN.
   OTHERWISE, I JUST MAY FEEL HOPELESS
         AND WITHOUT ANY REDEEMING VALUE.
   IF I FEEL REALLY UNWORTHY,
   LOOKING AT MY FAILINGS IS A TRIP TO
   THE OPERATING ROOM WITHOUT ANAESTHESIA.

3) **I HAVE TO TAKE IT OUT!**
   RECOGNIZING THIS, OWNING IT,
   AND THEN LETTING GO OF THIS,
   FREES ME FROM MY MISSILE SYSTEM.
   (ANYWAY, I FIND MY MISSILES END UP RETURNING
   AND LANDING ON MY **OWN** FRONT PORCH)
   WHEN I EXTRACT THE WORD "YOU"
       FROM MY HEATED STATE OF BEING,
       I FIND OUT THAT "I" AM ANGRY AND FRUSTRATED,
         THAT "I" AM UPSET ABOUT MANY THINGS..
         THAT HAVE NOTHING TO DO WITH HER...
         AND EVERYTHING TO DO WITH ME.
         AND I FIND THAT "I" HAVE IGNORED
           MY OWN SOUL.
         AND THAT MAYBE MY DISCONTENT IS
         "MY" SOUL CRYING OUT TO BE HEARD.

AND THIS JUST WON'T GO AWAY,
EVEN IF I DRIVE MY WIFE & FRIEND AWAY.
IS MY SOUL CONTENT
TO LET EVERYONE BE DISTANCED,
SO THAT "I" WILL FINALLY COME BACK
TO "MYSELF"...?

I DROP MY ATTACK, AND MY ATTITUDE,
AND BEGIN TO RETURN TO MYSELF. I COME HOME.

4) **OWNING OUR LOG** .
THIS BRINGS US BACK TO OUR SOUL AND
OPENS OUR VISION AGAIN.
JESUS SAYS WE ARE ABLE TO "SEE NOW".
NOW WE ARE NOT STANDING ON A CHAIR
LOOKING DOWN AT SOMEONE,
BUT WE ARE ON THE FLOOR,
ON THE SAME LEVEL, EYE **TO** EYE,
NOT EYE **FOR** EYE.
NOW WE CAN SEE SOMEONE ELSE......
WITH SOFTER EYES.

WHEN I TEACH THIS, I HAVE A 4 BY 4 BEAM
"STUCK" IN MY EYE,
SO I CAN'T SEE ANYTHING AT ALL.
WHEN I OWN MY DARKNESS, I DROP
THE BEAM AND NOW I BEGIN TO SEE.
BUT I ALSO **DON'T PUT THE BEAM AWAY**.
I PUT IT UNDER MY ARM,
SO I JOURNEY NOW **WITH THIS AWARENESS**.
I CAN'T BE TOO "**GOOD**" WITH THIS REMINDER UNDER MY ARM.
IT'S ALSO HARD TO BE "ARROGANT"
OR SELF-RIGHTEOUS NOW.

THEN I DON'T MEET ANYONE REALLY "**BENEATH**" ME.

EVERYONE LIKE ME HAS "DARKNESS", THEIR OWN LOG.
SOME KNOW IT, SOME DON'T.

I CAN RECEIVE EVERYONE
WITH HOSPITALITY, EQUINAMITY, WITHOUT JUDGMENT.
THIS CAN PROTECT ME FROM
ONE OF THE GREATEST SOUL DANGERS:
THAT OF FEELING HOLY, PURE, ELEVATED,
INFLATED, RIGHTEOUS, GOOD....

JESUS WAS APPROACHED WITH THE WORDS,
    "*GOOD TEACHER...*"
    JESUS RESPONDED,
    "DON'T CALL ME GOOD,
      NO ONE IS GOOD BUT GOD ALONE".   MARK 10:18

5) BY OWNING OUR DARKNESS
   WE WILL BE ABLE TO SEE AND
     ACTUALLY ABLE TO HELP OTHERS.
   WITH THE LOG UNDER OUR ARM,
     WE ARE HUMBLED,
      BUT ALSO WE CAN BE VERY USEFUL.
   WE CAN SEE CLEARLY NOW ,
     AND WITHOUT JUDGMENT.
   NO LONGER ARROGANT AND
     A REAL MIGRANE TO OTHERS,
     WE CAN OFFER ACCEPTANCE,
     MAYBE EVEN WISDOM.
   AND ALL WISDOM COMES FROM GOD.
   SO WE CAN BE AN INSTRUMENT OF
     DIVINE GRACE & WISDOM.
  HOW ABOUT THAT!

AND ALL PROCEEDING FROM THE
    COURAGE TO SEE,
         FACE, AND
         OWN OUR OWN DARKNESS!

WHAT HAPPENED TO PERFECTION?

THERE IS A BIBLE VERSE WE HAVE TO DEAL WITH:

"*BE YE THEREFORE PERFECT, EVEN AS*
 YOUR FATHER IN HEAVEN IS PERFECT."
                              MATTHEW 5:48 KJV

THIS IS A REAL PROBLEM FOR THIS "DARKNESS" ISSUE WE HAVE.
I THINK THIS IS THE WORST TRANSLATION IN THE WHOLE BIBLE.

JESUS SAW THAT "PERFECTION"
    (THE SUPPOSED RIGHTEOUSNESS OF THE GOOD ONES)
    WAS NOT ONLY **IMPOSSIBLE,**
    BUT **DANGEROUS TO THE SOUL**.

THE PROBLEM IS IN THE TRANSLATION
    OF THE GREEK WORD: *"TELIOS"*.
    THE KING JAMES VERSION (AND OTHERS)
    TAKE THAT TO BE "PERFECT".
    WHAT IT REALLY MEANS IS TO
    "BE BROUGHT TO COMPLETION"
     OR " TO EVOLVE WITHOUT CONSTRAINT",
     OR "TO GROW WITHOUT HINDRANCE".

SO WE CAN TRANSLATE THIS:

    "*SO EVOLVE,*
     COME INTO YOUR DESTINY,
     JUST AS GOD DOES."

NOW JESUS COULD SAY THAT.

AND WE CAN BE REALISTICALLY CHALLENGED BY THAT,
    AND AVOID ALL THAT NEUROTIC "PERFECTIONISM".

REFLECTIONS ON THE 3RD PRACTICE

"THE 1ST CHILD" A POEM

"IF I CANNOT SEE YOUR HUMANITY,
       I BEGIN TO FEAR YOU
     AND I SEE YOU AS AN ADVERSARY

AND YOU ONLY SEE "THAT",
    NOTHING ELSE.

AND WE TAKE UP RESIDENCE ON A BATTLEGROUND

ALL OF US, "INNOCENT",
TURNED INTO SOLDIERS
IN A WAR NO ONE WANTED
AND ALL REGRETTED

WE WAITED TO HEAR THE NAMES
OF THE FIRST VICTIMS

AND THE BIRTH
    OF THEIR FIRST CHILD,
      'VENGEANCE.'"

"THE DOWNWARD TURN"

WHEN WE FEEL *DOWN*:
    SAD, DISAPPOINTED, REGRETFUL, SHAMEFUL, GUILTY,
    RESENTFUL, GRIEVING OUR LOST HEALTH, YOUTH OR
    OPPORTUNITIES, OR FEARFUL OF THE FUTURE....
WE MAY GO TWO WAYS WITH THIS:

COUNTERACT IT   WITH "COUNT YOUR BLESSINGS",
    "PUT ON A HAPPY FACE", "DON'T LET IT GET YOU DOWN",
    OR EVEN ACTIVITIES THAT MAKE US FEEL BETTER,
    LIKE MUSIC, EXERCISE, TAKING A WALK.....
NUMB IT   WITH DISTRACTIONS LIKE TELEVISION OR VIDEO
    GAMES OR BUSYWORK ;
    COMPULSIONS LIKE SHOPPING, OR THE INTERNET;
    OR TRYING ON A COUPLE OF DRINKS...
       OR YOUR FAVORITE ANAESTETIC.
BUT THERE IS A 3RD WAY.
    YOU CAN GO *DOWN INTO IT*.

INSTEAD OF RUNNING AWAY, WALK TOWARD THIS.
ALLOW YOURSELF TO FULLY FEEL IT.
GO DOWN THE CORRIDORS OF SHAME & PAIN.
GO TO THE ROOM WHERE IT RESIDES.
INVITE THE SPIRIT OF GOD TO GO WITH YOU.
    OPEN THE DOOR...
    GO IN AND ENTER INTO THE SCENE.
    IT MAY BE FROZEN IN TIME.
    LET IT THAW OUT....

    RELIVE IT IF IT HAS BEEN WAITING FOR YOU.
    IT'S THERE FOR A REASON.
    FEEL THE GRIEF & PAIN THERE.
    ALLOW IT TO <u>FLOW INTO YOU</u> ...
        AND <u>THROUGH YOU</u>...
            AND THEN <u>RELEASE IT</u> WHEN IT IS TIME...

WHEN THIS HAS BEEN RELEASED,
    COME BACK INTO REAL TIME.
REFLECT ON WHAT THIS MEANS......

WHAT DOES THIS TEACH YOU ABOUT YOURSELF...
            ABOUT YOUR WORLD?

WHAT GIFT DOES IT BRING TO YOU?
    EXPRESS IT IN WRITING, ART, OR MUSIC...
    DOES IT BRING YOU INTO A NEW FORM OF EXPRESSION?

WHEN YOU FIND YOURSELF FEELING "DOWN" AGAIN,
    TAKE THE "DOWNWARD TURN"
    AND <u>GO INTO IT</u>....

<u>**WE SEE JESUS PRACTICING THIS**</u> WHEN HE GOES ALONE
    INTO THE DESERT TO ENTER INTO DARK NIGHTS OF
    SOUL STRUGGLE AND HEALING, AND DAYS OF FORMATION.
    WE SEE HIM GO INTO THIS <u>FULLY</u>,
    INVITING THE SPIRIT OF GOD TO GO WITH HIM.
    WE SEE HIM TRAVELING LIGHTER AFTER THIS:
    NOT AFRAID OF THE FUTURE AND
    NOT CARRYING AROUND ROOMS HEAVY WITH THE PAST.

JESUS CONTINUES THROUGH HIS LIFE
    TO ENTER INTO THE DAWN AND THE DUSK
    COMPANIONED BY THE SPIRIT
    TO FACE &
    OWN THE DARKNESS.

SONG OF THE BELOVED

IN JOHN 13:3 JESUS CONVEYS TO HIS COMMUNITY HIS SPIRITUALITY IN A POETIC IMAGE AS HE GETS UP TO WASH THEIR FEET IN A PROFOUND CEREMONY.

"JESUS KNEW THAT ABBA HAD PUT
EVERYTHING INTO HIS HANDS, AND THAT
HE HAD COME FROM GOD AND
WAS RETURNING TO GOD,
AND HE GOT UP FROM THE TABLE..."

I HAVE PUT THIS INTO
A **CHANT** THAT CAN BE SUNG TO THE TUNE "DIVINUM MYSTERIUM" ("OF THE FATHER'S LOVE BEGOTTEN"), OR CAN BE DONE WITH THE **MOVEMENTS** INDICATED, OR CAN BE SIMPLY DONE AS A **BREATHING PRAYER** WHEREVER YOU ARE...

OUTBREATH:	"I HAVE COME FROM THE BELOVED,	HANDS MOVE DOWN
INBREATH:	TO THE BELOVED I RETURN	HANDS RAISE UP
OUTBREATH:	I AM HELD WITHIN THE HOLY ONE	ARMS LOWER IN EMBRACE OF SELF
INBREATH:	AND THE SPIRIT'S POWER IS HERE."	HANDS GATHER TO HEART

REFLECTION:

IF YOU KNEW THAT YOU HAVE **COME FROM GOD**
AND THAT YOU WOULD **RETURN TO GOD**
AND THAT GOD HAD PLACED **EVERYTHING YOU NEED**
INTO YOUR HANDS.......

WHAT WOULD YOU DO WITH YOUR LIFE?

WHO WOULD YOU DARE TO BE?

THE OUTWARD JOURNEY

THE 1ST THREE PRACTICES
    ARE THE INWARD JOURNEY OF JESUS.
THIS WAS THE PART **HARD TO SEE** IN JESUS' LIFE.
    HE GOES OUT INTO THE DARK NIGHT TO BE ALONE.
    HE WITHDRAWS IN THE DIM DAWN.
    BUT HIS LIFE POURS FORTH FROM THIS INWARD LIFE.

THE 4TH PRACTICE BEGINS THE OUTWARD JOURNEY.
THE PART YOU BEGIN TO **SEE**.

YOU COULD SAY THAT THE SPRING OF LIVING WATER THAT
        FLOWS FROM **WITHIN** JESUS
        FLOWS OUT
    AS A RIVER OF BLESSING TO OTHERS.
YOU COULD SAY THAT
    JESUS BREATHES **IN** THE BREATH OF GOD, AND THEN
        BREATHES IT **OUT** TO PEOPLE AROUND.
YOU COULD SAY THAT THE STRUGGLE
        INSIDE JESUS THAT IS SO EMPOWERING FOR HIM,
    FLOWS **OUT** AS A POWER TO EN-COURAGE US TO
        LIVE **INTO** OUR STRUGGLE.
AFTER ALL, THE WORD "ISRA_EL_" MEANS TO WRESTLE WITH
    GOD "EL".

SO THE INWARD JOURNEY ISSUES FORTH
    INTO AN OUTWARD ONE.
    YOU CAN TRUST THAT.

MAYBE THE MEANING OF OUR LIFE IS ON HOLD
    UNTIL WE BEGIN AN INWARD JOURNEY.
        THEN THAT COULD
            ISSUE FORTH INTO AN **OUTWARD LIFE**
            THAT WE ALWAYS BELIEVED
                THAT WE WERE MEANT TO LIVE,
                BUT HADN'T KNOWN HOW TO
                BEGIN.

"It is spring in 2008. I am listening to a woman who is drowning in a pool of shame. Being active in church, hearing the absolution of sin, serving others has not touched this illness.
*   The pervasive illness of shame afflicts almost everyone who has come into my "confession box" in the last 40 years.*
*   If sin is doing something "bad" and feeling guilt,*
*   shame is feeling like a "bad person".*
*   Sin can be forgiven, absolved, but shame can't be forgiven.*

It just doesn't go away in time.
Is that why the inner life is so hard for this woman?
   Who wants to sit <u>alone</u> in a pool of shame?
   Shame must be healed, not forgiven.
   And unconditional love heals shame.
This woman's illness needs compassion, the subtle,
   but great power of the universe."

THE 4TH PRACTICE: <u>BE COMPASSIONATE</u>

"BE COMPASSIONATE AS YOUR BELOVED CREATOR IS COMPASSIONATE."
LUKE 6:36

IF THE 2ND PRACTICE IMMERSES US
   IN THE <u>**SPRINGS OF DIVINE COMPASSION**</u>,
AND THE 3RD PRACTICE FREES US
   TO <u>**SEE OTHER PEOPLE**</u> (& FELLOW SPECIES),
THEN IN OUR SEEING WE CAN BEGIN
   TO <u>**FEEL EMPATHY**</u>,
      <u>**CONNECTION WITHOUT JUDGMENT**</u>,
         AND SOMETHING CAN
           <u>**FLOW OUT**</u>
            <u>**THROUGH ME**</u>
              <u>**TOWARD OTHERS**</u>.

THIS DOES SOUND LIKE PLUMBING,
   BUT THIS IS THE MYSTERIOUS HEALING JUICE OF LIFE.
   THIS IS THE <u>**DIVINE LOVE THAT RESIDES WITHIN EVERYONE**</u>.
      EVERY CELL, PLANT, STAR, MOLECULE
         COMES OUT OF THIS <u>**INDWELLING ENERGY**</u>.
     IT IS THE <u>**RADIANCE WITHIN ALL THINGS**</u>.
     IT IS THE <u>BEAUTY</u> OF THE DAWN SKY,
     THE DEEP BLUE OF THE <u>VIOLET PETAL</u>,
     THE <u>LAUGHTER OF CHILDREN</u>,
     THE WARMTH IN THE <u>FACE OF JESUS</u>.
     IT FILLS THE HEART WITH <u>JOY</u> AND MAKES US <u>SMILE</u>.
     IT IS IN THE 4 YEAR OLDS <u>LONGING TO PLAY</u> WITH YOU.
     IT IS THE <u>WAGGING OF A TAIL</u>.

AND GET THIS. WE ARE PRIVILEGED
      TO DELIVER THIS <u>**DIVINE ENERGY TO OTHERS**</u>
     JUST AS IT IS <u>**DELIVERED FRESH TO US**</u>.
AND IT FEELS SO SIGNIFICANT AND FULFILLING AND HEALING
      TO BE A <u>**PART**</u> OF SUCH AN EPIPHANY.
      WHAT GREATER HONOR IS THERE?

How can we "Be Compassionate"?

If it is in our nature to be so,
how do we encourage this to flow through our life?
Here are **three reflections** on this:

1) **BE HERE NOW**!

Disconnect
from our cultural busyness & distraction!
When I disregard my chronic time crunch,
abandon my agenda,
I can be **PRESENT**, here & now.
I can pay attention.

I was talking with a truck-driver on the road,
and was **NOT** in a hurry.
I was amazed in a few minutes what I began
to feel for this man's life and family.
This relaxation of being allows me
to be actually **WITH** another person.

This is momentous when that one
is someone very nearby...
the one most likely
to be taken for granted... or not seen.

Jesus abandons his agenda of teaching
to just be with the children..... playing,
laughing with them, loving them joyfully.
He didn't have children himself,
but **THEN** he did.
The disciples were upset with the interruption
because their anxiety/distraction
closed their hearts, leaving them disconnected,
irritated... and very absent.

MEDITATION:
Take a full, rich breath......

and FALL... (as into the river...)
FALL DEEPLY
INTO THIS MOMENT
OF GRACE

2) ENTERTAIN ANGELS

In Genesis 18, Abraham greets three strangers
    with **GREAT HOSPITALITY**: washing feet,
    offering water, rest, and a mid-day feast.
    This act of compassion turned into
    his lucky day, for they were
    MESSENGERS OF THE HOLY ONE.

In Matthew 25, the one who visited the prisoner,
    fed the hungry one, came to the sick one,
    was **SHOCKED TO FIND OUT** that it was **"CHRIST"**
    who they had actually visited, fed.....

So YOU NEVER REALLY KNOW WHO YOU ARE WITH!!

In fact, Paul in Galatians 2:20 even says,
    "It is no longer I who live,
    but Christ who lives in me!"

So there is something noumenous in ordinary encounters!

Then, why not hold on to the prospect
    That this is indeed a mysterious place we inhabit
    and begin the entertainment... of angels...
    maybe the angel we entertain will turn out to be...
    ourselves!

Might that help us to **STOP,**
    PAY ATTENTION,
    and **OPEN OUR HEART**
    to those we meet on our path.

I have found it a delight to **TALK TO STRANGERS**.
    Rarely am I rebuffed, and if so,
    I don't take it personally...they don't know me.
        Almost always people smile,
        talk back,
        even open up.
        Sometimes tears come as we connect
        and tell our stories.
        That is **HOLY GROUND**.

When this happens I find we carry a
        SECRET "KINSHIP" with each other.

And I begin to feel part of
     a **LARGER FAMILY** and
     MORE AT HOME WHEREVER I AM.
Actually we might even go **OFF** our path
to meet someone...

*"But a Samaritan traveler who came on him
was moved with compassion **WHEN HE SAW** him."*
                                        Luke 10:33
This is the story of a Jewish man wounded
on the side of the road. He had a Samaritan man
(Jews & Samaritans hated each other)
SEE him in his suffering and become the **"ANGEL"**
he so desperately needed.

3)COMMON GROUND

The 3rd practice (facing/owning our darkness)
   can help us here.

I mentioned that I use a 4" by 4" beam to illustrate.
   I take the beam out of my eye,
      and then I can **SEE** someone else.
   But then I put the 4 by 4 under my arm
      and take it with me.
   It reminds me of my own darkness and vulnerability
      LEST I FORGET!

And when **I FORGET,**
   I will want to look **"GOOD"**
   and then I will begin to **"ASCEND"**.
   After that I start to **LOOK DOWN** on you,
   and then I get **JUDGMENTAL** &
   CRITICAL of **YOUR** failures,
   YOUR limitations, **YOUR** darkness.
   The 4 by 4 reminds me of **MYSELF** ,
   so I can abandon arrogance, class distinction,
   economic power, educational superiority, etc.

   STANDING ON COMMON GROUND
   with my 4 by 4 under my arm,
   I can begin **TO FEEL**
   the ruggedness of **YOUR** journey,
      the boulders, the climb, the fall........
   Then you become **REAL** to me, my eyes soften,

I WARM UP, MY FACE THAWS.
   I HEAR YOUR STORY. I SHARE SOME OF MINE.
   WE CONNECT. THERE IS NO JUDGMENT.
   THERE IS A FREE SPACE
         IN WHICH TO BREATHE, TO RELAX.
   WE BOTH KNOW OUR VULNERABILITY, OUR CHALLENGE.
   THERE IS FREEDOM & TENDERNESS HERE...
   WE ARE ON COMMON... AND HOLY GROUND.
   THERE IS A ***PRESENCE*** HERE TOO.

THERE IS A GREAT JOY IN BEING ONE'S **ENTIRE** SELF.
MY VULNERABILITY, MY DARKNESS
NEVER WILL BE GONE!

I WILL NOT IN THIS LIFE ASCEND BEYOND IT.
I AM NOT **ABOVE** **ANYONE**.
THIS TRUTH MAY BE DISHEARTENING
   TO THOSE "UPWARDLY" MOBILE IN SPIRIT,
BUT ACTUALLY THIS
               DESCENDING ONTO
                  COMMON GROUND
                     IS A GREAT GIFT.
IT ALLOWS ME TO HAVE COMPASSION,
   AND IF THAT IS THE HIGHEST VALUE,
   THE TRIUMPH OF THE HUMAN SPECIES,
   THEN BRING IT ON.

ST. FRANCIS OF ASSISI SAID HE LEARNED
   THAT HE WAS CAPABLE OF ANY ACT,
   AND THEREFORE HE WAS FREE OF JUDGMENT,
   AND CAPABLE OF COMPASSION TOWARD ALL. [11]
   (AND THERE ARE STATUES OF **HIM** EVERYWHERE)

IF **MY** VULNERABILITY & **MY** BROKENNESS
   IS THE WAY TO COMPASSION,
   I WILL CELEBRATE **EVEN THAT**... ESP. THAT!

IF THE **WAY OF COMPASSION** IS THE WAY
   TO YOKE WITH THE WORK OF GOD IN THIS TIME,
   THEN **LET IT BE MY WAY**.

   WHAT WOULD BE GREATER THAN TO PARTNER
   IN THE GREAT WORK OF GOD?
   WHAT COULD TRUMP THAT?

AND WE WILL ALWAYS RETURN
      TO THE 2ND PRACTICE (IMMERSION IN GRACE)
      AND LET COMPASSION FLOOD OUR OWN BEING
      WITH GOD'S GRACE, SELF-FORGIVENESS, AND
      SELF-TENDERNESS.
      THE HEALING WATERS FLOW INTO OUR VERY SELF.
      THIS FILLING WITH GRACE EMBRACES
      ALL OUR FLAWS AND FAILURES
      AND IS THAT GRACE
         THAT VERY SAME GRACE THAT
            FLOWS OUT TO OTHERS
               IN HEALING COMPASSION.
IT BEGINS IN **GOD'S** HEART.
    & FLOWS INTO **MY** HEART
       & FLOWS **OUT IN EVERY DIRECTION.**
   NOT BECAUSE I'M GOOD, OR DEDICATED,
   OR STRIVING HARD, OR LIKE PEOPLE,
      OR AM SPIRITUAL, OR A CHRISTIAN...
IT IS THE NATURE OF GOD & IT IS MY NATURE.
I HAVE SURRENDERED TO MY OWN BEING.

MEDITATION:

Image someone that you struggle with......

Reflect:

   "What is it like to be you?".......
      (Put yourself entirely into their skin)...

   "What are your fears, pain, anger"...?

   "What do you love"...?

   " What do you long for"...?

   Can you find common ground?......

THOUGHTS ON "SURRENDERED LOVE" & THE WAY OF JESUS

THE WAY OF JESUS WAS
      A DANGEROUS PATH TO THE WAY OF CONVENTION,
      TO THE EGO-CENTRIC EGO,
      AND A LOT OF OUR OWN WELL-LAID PLANS.
      IT WAS THE **PATH OF SURRENDERED LOVE**.
      SURRENDERED LOVE IS A LOT LIKE FALLING IN LOVE.
      IT IS **TRANSFORMING**...
          TAKES US OUT OF
          OUR LITTLE SHRINK-WRAPPED WORLD
             AND **SEES** THE WORLD AFRESH...
             WE **IMAGINE** WE ARE MORE...
             KNOW THAT WE ARE LOVED.

IT BREAKS THE HEART OPEN LIKE A **SEED,**
      AND WE KNOW WHAT CAN HAPPEN WITH A SEED...
      ROOTS GROPE DOWN INTO MOIST DARK SOIL
          (A METAPHOR FOR ONE'S INWARD JOURNEY).
      SHOOTS GO UPWARD TOWARD THE LIGHT OF THE SUN
          (METAPHOR FOR ONE'S OUTWARD JOURNEY).

WE WERE A SEED BUT THERE WAS **MORE**
THAT WE WERE TO BE:
      ROOTS & SHOOTS... AND EVEN MORE TO COME...
      BLOSSOMS...   FRUIT...
      AND THEN BEYOND OUR IMAGININGS,
      A FRUITED TREE.

JESUS' IMAGE OF THE REIGN OF GOD WAS A SEED...
      THAT JUST NEEDED TO BE **CRACKED OPEN**.
      THEN A TRANSFORMATION WOULD TAKE PLACE
          THAT WOULD AMAZE ALL.

MARY AND JOHN FELL IN LOVE WITH JESUS
      AND THAT SURRENDERED LOVE
          WOULD CRACK THEM OPEN.
      WE KNOW THEY WERE ESPECIALLY CLOSE TO JESUS.
      WE DON'T GET TO SEE **THEIR** TRANSFORMATION
         IN THE GOSPELS,

      BUT WE DO GET TO SEE MORE ABOUT WHAT HAPPENS
      WHEN YOU **CAN'T** SURRENDER TO LOVE.

AND THAT IS SIMON PETER
          AND THE OTHER DISCIPLES' STRUGGLE.

FOR US IT MAY BE A FRIEND OR TEACHER THAT WE **TRUST**.
          ONE WHO **EMBODIES THE DIVINE LOVE**... INCARNATES IT.
          OUR TRANSFORMATION IS OUR GROWING TRUST
                    IN **THEIR LOVE**,
          LETTING IT SOAK INTO OUR PORES AND THEN CELLS.

*THIS CRACKING OPEN ALLOWS US TO BEGIN
          TO FEEL A LARGER LOVE
                    COULD BE EMBRACING US:
                              THE LOVE OF THE DIVINE BELOVED.*

*CAN IT BE THAT THE DIVINE LOVER
          HAS REACHED US
          THROUGH THIS TRUSTED & LOVING FRIEND?*

THEY HAVE BECOME **THE INSTRUMENT**
          THAT THE SPIRIT HAS BLOWN THROUGH.
          WE HAVE FALLEN IN LOVE WITH THIS MUSIC
                    AND THIS MUSIC IS HEALING OUR SOUL.

IT IS IMPORTANT FOR **US** TO REALIZE THAT THIS MUSIC
          HAS COME **THROUGH THEM**.
          THEY ARE NOT THE MUSIC, THEY ARE THE INSTRUMENT.

WE WANT TO FALL INTO THIS MUSIC,
          FROM THE **BREATH OF THE BELOVED**,
                    THE HEART OF GOD.

(IF YOU ARE THE FRIEND/TEACHER
   WHO HAS BEEN THE INSTRUMENT
   THAT THIS MUSIC HAS COME THROUGH,
   IT'S IMPORTANT FOR YOU TO NOT IMAGINE
   THAT YOU **ARE** THE MUSIC.
   THEN YOU CAN REALLY
   ENJOY BEING AN INSTRUMENT.
   I THINK PART OF THE GENIUS
  OF JESUS IS THAT HE LOVED THE MUSIC
   SO MUCH THAT IT WAS ENOUGH
   TO BE THE INSTRUMENT
   IN THE BELOVED'S HANDS.)

WHEN COMPASSION GETS *TOUGH*, EVEN FOR JESUS

"JESUS LEFT THAT PLACE AND WENT AWAY TO THE DISTRICT OF TYRE
AND SIDON. JUST THEN A CANAANITE WOMAN FROM THAT REGION
CAME OUT AND STARTED SHOUTING,
> 'HAVE MERCY ON ME, LORD, SON OF DAVID;
> MY DAUGHTER IS TORMENTED BY A DEMON.'
BUT HE DID NOT ANSWER HER AT ALL.
AND HIS DISCIPLES CAME AND URGED HIM, SAYING,
> 'SEND HER AWAY,
> FOR SHE KEEPS SHOUTING AFTER US.'
HE ANSWERED,
> 'I WAS SENT ONLY TO THE LOST SHEEP
> OF THE HOUSE OF ISRAEL.'
BUT SHE CAME AND KNELT BEFORE HIM SAYING,
> 'LORD, HELP ME'.
 HE ANSWERED,
> 'IT IS NOT FAIR TO TAKE THE CHILDREN'S FOOD
> AND THROW IT TO THE DOGS.'
SHE SAID,
> 'YES, LORD, YET EVEN THE DOGS EAT THE CRUMBS
> THAT FALL FROM THE MASTER'S TABLE.'
THEN JESUS ANSWERED HER,
> 'WOMAN, GREAT IS YOUR FAITH!'
> LET IT BE DONE FOR YOU AS YOU WISH.'
AND HER DAUGHTER WAS HEALED INSTANTLY."

MATTHEW 15:21-28

HERE WE FEEL THE PRESENCE OF WHAT JESUS HAS BEEN
TAUGHT ALL HIS LIFE AND THE WEIGHT OF TRADITION.
JEWS WERE NOT TO TALK TO SAMARITANS, THEIR CLOSE
KIN, LET ALONE CANAANITES WHO WERE GENTILE AND
POLYTHEISTIC. THEY WERE CALLED "DOGS".
MEN WERE NOT TO TALK TO OR TOUCH WOMEN EITHER.
THIS HELPED TO DISCOURAGE INTER-MARRIAGE AND
ADULTERATION OF THE FAITH.

JESUS' CONCEPT OF HIS MISSION WAS ALSO
ONLY TO ISRAEL'S LOST, EXCLUDING HER.

YOU MIGHT SAY THAT THERE WERE GOOD REASONS
JEWS HAD A 4 BY 4 BEAM IN THEIR EYES
THAT PREVENTED THEM FROM **SEEING** GENTILES.
GENTILES HAD THE BEAM TOO.
NOT MUCH COULD HAPPEN BETWEEN THEM.

YET, NOTICE HOW THE
      WOMAN **SEES** JESUS,
      SEES THE **POWER** WITHIN JESUS
      (SEES THE **DIVINE**?).
   SHE SAYS KNEELING, "*LORD, HELP ME.*"
        (ANCIENT "KYRIE ELEISON" OF CHURCH'S LITURGY).

JESUS BEGINS TO FEEL **SEEN** NOW,
      AND HE STATES HOW HE IS
      CAUGHT IN HIS TRADITION & TEACHING,
      "*IT IS NOT FAIR TO TAKE THE CHILDREN'S FOOD*
          AND THROW IT TO THE DOGS...".

BUT SHE WILL NOT LET THAT STOP HER.
      SHE IS HUNGRY FOR GRACE,
      AND EVEN DOGS NEED THIS GRACE.
JESUS REALLY SEES HER NOW
      AND THE **DIVINE LONGING** IN HER
      THAT HE SOUGHT TO FIND IN SO MANY...
      AND DIDN'T.

AND THERE IS A **GREAT FLOWING OF COMPASSION**,
      A HEALING ENERGY, TOWARD HER THROUGH JESUS.
      IN THE MOST AWKWARD OF CIRCUMSTANCES
      THIS COMPASSION FLOWS.
      THIS HEALS THE DAUGHTER.
      THIS FILLS THE CANAANITE WOMAN
      WITH DIVINE BLESSING AND JOY.

AND JESUS' CULTURAL BIAS ABOUT GENTILES FALLS AWAY,
      HIS WORLD EXPANDS,
      AND HIS MISSION IS BLOWN OPEN.
HOW VULNERABLE JESUS IS:
TO BE TAUGHT, TRANSFORMED BY A GENTILE WOMAN! AMAZING!!!

IN ALL THIS EXCITEMENT,
   YOU CAN BARELY HEAR THE SOUND OF THE WALL
    COME
     DOWN
      BETWEEN JEWS & GENTILES.

   AND JESUS WAS NOT THE SAME.

THE 5TH PRACTICE: CREATE SPIRITUAL COMMUNITY

"It is 2002. I discover that three people that have shaped my life:
Thich Nhat Hanh, a Vietnamese Buddhist monk;
Martin Luther King, a Baptist minister; and
Thomas Merton, a Catholic monk were friends.
Martin's engagement for racial justice influenced Thich as he extended his practice to compassionate, non-violent "engaged Buddhism".
Thich's work for peace in Viet Nam influenced Martin to come out against the war in Viet Nam, a costly position.
And both of them affected Thomas as he opened his Christianity to the wisdom of the East and to the struggle for justice.
Martin and Thomas surely brought Thich to look deeply into the compassionate and prophetic way of Jesus.
Martin & Thomas both died in 1968. Thich lives on richly.
This unlikely trio had "Spiritual Community" and empowered each other, and also many of us."

"AS JESUS WAS WALKING ALONG BY THE LAKE OF GALILEE, HE SAW SIMON AND HIS BROTHER ANDREW CASTING A NET IN THE LAKE... AND JESUS SAID,
'COME AFTER ME AND I WILL MAKE YOU INTO
FISHERS FOR PEOPLE'. AND AT ONCE THEY LEFT THEIR
NETS AND FOLLOWED HIM.'   MARK 1:16F

THE SMALL COMMUNITY THAT JESUS CREATED
WAS ESSENTIAL TO THE SPIRIT-MOVEMENT OF JESUS.
IT WAS ESSENTIAL FOR HIS OWN SUPPORT.
IT WAS A NEW FAMILY.
IT WAS FOUNDATIONAL FOR HIS FOLLOWERS
TO LIVE AS A COMMUNITY,
BUT ALSO TO LIVE AS A TRAVELING "SCHOOL"...
A PLACE TO **LEARN & PRACTICE** THE NEW PATH.
AND IT WAS ESSENTIAL FOR THE WORLD
FOR THIS WAS THE *"CRUCIBLE"*,
THE CONTAINER FOR THE NEW LIFE.
AND AFTER JESUS LEFT,
THEY WOULD BE THE CONTAINER...
AND THE LIGHT, SEED, LEAVEN, & SALT.

THERE WAS A LOT AT STAKE IN THAT SMALL, UNEDUCATED,
UNFORMED SLICE OF MIDDLE-EASTERN COMMON FOLK.
DID ANYONE REALIZE THE STAKES?

IF SO MUCH DEPENDS ON THIS,
        JUST **_WHAT IS SPIRITUAL COMMUNITY?_**
    LET'S LOOK AT IT THROUGH THESE **SIX LENSES**:

1)THE NEW FAMILY

"...HE MADE HIS WAY THROUGH VILLAGES PREACHING & PROCLAIMING THE GOOD NEWS OF THE KINGDOM OF GOD. WITH HIM WENT THE TWELVE, AS WELL AS CERTAIN WOMEN WHO HAD BEEN CURED OF EVIL SPIRITS AND AILMENTS:
  MARY SURNAMED THE MAGDALENE,
    FROM WHOM SEVEN DEMONS HAD GONE OUT,
  JOANNA, THE WIFE OF HEROD'S STEWARD CHUZA,
  SUSANNA, AND MANY OTHERS WHO PROVIDED FOR THEM
    OUT OF THEIR OWN RESOURCES..."   LUKE 8:1-3

"(JESUS') MOTHER AND HIS BROTHERS ARRIVED AND
  STANDING OUTSIDE, SENT IN A MESSAGE ASKING FOR HIM.
  A CROWD WAS SITTING ROUND HIM AT THE TIME THE
  MESSAGE WAS PASSED TO HIM,
    'LOOK, YOUR MOTHER AND BROTHERS AND SISTERS
    ARE OUTSIDE ASKING FOR YOU.'
AND LOOKING AT THOSE SITTING IN A CIRCLE ROUND HIM,
HE SAID,
    'HERE ARE MY MOTHER AND MY BROTHERS.
    ANYONE WHO DOES THE WILL OF GOD, THAT PERSON IS
    MY BROTHER AND SISTER AND MOTHER.'"   MARK 3: 31-35

OR: *"MY MOTHER AND MY BROTHERS ARE THOSE WHO*
        HEAR THE WORD OF GOD AND DO IT."
                                PARALLEL IN LUKE 8:21

THE "GOOD NEWS OF THE REIGN OF GOD"
        SOUNDS SO ABSTRACT & PHILOSOPHICAL.
        BUT IT WAS TO BECOME VERY VISIBLE NOW.

IF YOU COULDN'T IMAGINE IT, DON'T WORRY, **_HERE IT IS_**!
    IT **LOOKS** LIKE A CROWD LISTENING TO THE WORD OF GOD.
    IT **LOOKS** LIKE WOMEN & MEN TOGETHER IN COMMUNITY
        THOUGH SEPARATED BY TRADITION & RELIGION.
    IT **LOOKS** LIKE SAMARITANS & JEWS LAUGHING TOGETHER
        AND TOUCHING WHEN THAT WAS PROHIBITED.
    IT **LOOKS** LIKE CRIMINALS, PROSTITUTES, AND HOLY MEN
        PASSING FOOD TO EACH OTHER AT DINNER,

IN SPITE OF RELIGIOUS ISSUES OF "UNCLEANNESS".
IT LOOKS LIKE A "NEW FAMILY".
NO ONE HAD CONCEIVED OF THIS,
    YET **HERE IT WAS.**

THIS NEW FAMILY WAS RADICALLY INCLUSIVE AND
    BROKE PRACTICALLY EVERY RULE ABOUT HOW PEOPLE
    COULD GET TOGETHER.
MAYBE IT HELPED THAT THIS WAS A
        COMMUNITY OF ***PRACTICE***, NOT PROFESSION.
THIS WAS A GATHERING NOT BASED
        ON CREED, BUT ON ***COMPASSION***,
        NOT ON PURITY, BUT ON ***GRACE***.

THIS NEW FAMILY WAS A "SIGHT TO BEHOLD".
IT WAS THE POWER OF COMPASSION TO **BRIDGE THE CHASMS**
        BETWEEN US: POOR/RICH, GENTILE/JEW,
        DARK/LIGHT SKIN, WOMAN/MAN,
        IMMIGRANT/CITIZEN, YOUNG/OLD,
        HOMOSEXUAL/HETEROSEXUAL,
        WHATEVER IT IS... IT CAN BRIDGE IT.
AND THIS NEW FAMILY HAS AN "ACE IN THE HOLE".

"IN TRUTH I TELL YOU AGAIN, IF TWO OF YOU ON EARTH
    AGREE TO ASK ANYTHING AT ALL,
    IT WILL BE GRANTED TO YOU BY "ABBA".
FOR WHERE TWO OR THREE GATHER TOGETHER IN MY NAME,
    I AM THERE AMONG THEM."   MATTHEW 18:19

AS WE DESCRIBED IN THE 1ˢᵀ SECTION
    ON THE SPIRITUALITY OF JESUS,
    THE **1ˢᵀ PROTOTYPE** OF THE REIGN OF GOD
    IS THE **TABLE OF JESUS**".

SO THE 5ᵀᴴ PRACTICE IS HOW
    COMPASSION (4ᵀᴴ PRACTICE)
    AND OUR VULNERABILITY AND LONGING
    CAN CREATE THIS "TABLE".
    AND IT WILL BE THE "NEW FAMILY" WE WILL NEED.

THIS "NEW FAMILY" IS ALSO A NURSERY
    FOR THE **"NEW HUMAN"** WHICH IS
    THE **2ᴺᴰ PROTOTYPE** OF THE REIGN OF GOD
                    (SEE 1ˢᵀ SECTION).
THE **NEW HUMAN** HAS TO START SOMEWHERE.

IT HAS A FRAGILE BEGINNING AND NEEDS MOMS & DADS,
    BROTHERS & SISTERS, UNCLES & AUNTS.
THERE NEEDS TO BE TIME AND A LOT OF GROWING,
    EVOLVING, SHEDDING OF SKINS... MANY MOLTS.
30 YEARS AFTER JESUS' DEATH,
    AN ELDER WRITES TO ONE OF THESE *NEW FAMILIES*
    TO COUNSEL/ENCOURAGE THEM:

" *YOU WERE TO PUT ASIDE YOUR OLD SELF,*
   WHICH BELONGS TO YOUR OLD WAY OF LIFE
   AND IS CORRUPTED BY FOLLOWING ILLUSORY DESIRES. YOUR MIND
WAS TO BE RENEWED IN SPIRIT.
SO THAT YOU COULD PUT ON THE "NEW HUMAN"
   THAT HAS BEEN CREATED ON GOD'S PRINCIPLES...
SO FROM NOW ON, THERE MUST BE NO MORE LIES.
   SPEAK THE TRUTH TO ONE ANOTHER,
   SINCE WE ARE ALL PARTS OF ONE ANOTHER...
NEVER LET THE SUN SET ON YOUR ANGER...
LET YOUR WORDS BE FOR THE IMPROVEMENT OF OTHERS.
ANY BITTERNESS OR BAD TEMPER OR ANGER OR
   SHOUTING OR ABUSE MUST BE FAR REMOVED FROM YOU —
   AS MUST EVERY KIND OF MALICE.
BE GENEROUS TO ONE ANOTHER, SYMPATHETIC,
   FORGIVING EACH OTHER AS READILY
   AS GOD FORGAVE YOU...
AS GOD'S DEAR CHILDREN, THEN, TAKE (CHRIST)
   AS YOUR PATTERN..."   EPHESIANS 4:22F.

2)THE SPIRIT- MOVEMENT

THE DYNAMICS OF SPIRITUAL COMMUNITY ARE SEEN
IN THIS STORY:

"THE APOSTLES REJOINED JESUS AND TOLD HIM ALL THEY HAD DONE
AND TAUGHT. AND HE SAID TO THEM,
   'COME AWAY TO SOME LONELY PLACE ALL BY YOURSELVES
   AND REST FOR A WHILE';
FOR THERE WERE SO MANY COMING AND GOING THAT THERE
   WAS NO TIME FOR THEM EVEN TO EAT.
SO THEY WENT OFF IN THE BOAT TO A LONELY PLACE WHERE THEY
COULD BE BY THEMSELVES."   MARK 6: 30-32

IT ALL BEGINS WITH THE 1ST PRACTICE.

THERE WILL BE NO SPIRITUAL COMMUNITY OF SIGNIFICANCE,
   LET ALONE POWER, **WITHOUT THE INWARD JOURNEY**.
THEY DID NOT HAVE THIS. **THEY** DIDN'T GO INTO THE DESERT. JESUS
HAD TO LEAD THEM OUT TO A "DESERTED" PLACE
   FOR REST, REJUVENATION, RENEWAL, AND EMPOWERING
   SOLITUDE, MEDITATION, AND PRAYER.
 THIS WAS JESUS' SPIRITUALITY. **IT WAS TO BE THEIRS**,
   BUT THE CROWD, LIKE OUR NEEDY & FRENETIC CULTURE,
   WOULDN'T HAVE IT.

"BUT PEOPLE SAW THEM GOING, AND MANY RECOGNIZED
   THEM; AND FROM EVERY TOWN THEY ALL HURRIED TO THE
   PLACE ON FOOT AND REACHED IT BEFORE THEM.
SO AS HE STEPPED ASHORE HE SAW A LARGE CROWD;
   AND HE TOOK PITY ON THEM BECAUSE THEY WERE
   LIKE SHEEP WITHOUT A SHEPHERD, AND HE SET HIMSELF
   TO TEACH THEM AT SOME LENGTH."   MARK 6: 33-34

THE PEOPLE LOOKED SO LOST THAT JESUS FELT THEIR
   DESPERATION, WAS FILLED WITH COMPASSION (4TH
   PRACTICE), AND BEGAN TO TEACH THEM.
NOTE HOW TEACHING COMES OUT OF
   REAL "SEEING" AND "FEELING".
   COMPASSION DRIVES THIS TEACHING, NOT DUTY.
THE "SHEEP WITHOUT A SHEPHERD" IMAGE IS STRONG IN THE
   HEBREW BIBLE. JESUS EXPERIENCES THIS AS A CALL TO
   STEP FORWARD... AND NOT JUST HIM,
   BUT ALSO HIS STUDENTS...

"BY NOW IT WAS GETTING VERY LATE, AND HIS DISCIPLES
   CAME UP TO HIM AND SAID,
    'THIS IS A LONELY PLACE AND IT IS GETTING VERY LATE,
    SO SEND THEM AWAY, AND THEY CAN GO TO THE FARMS
    AND VILLAGES ROUND ABOUT, TO BUY THEMSELVES
    SOMETHING TO EAT.' HE REPLIED,
    'GIVE THEM SOMETHING TO EAT YOURSELVES.'
THEY ANSWERED,
    'ARE WE TO GO AND SPEND TWO HUNDRED DENARII
    (200 DAY'S WAGE) ON BREAD FOR THEM TO EAT?'
HE ASKED, 'HOW MANY LOAVES HAVE YOU? GO AND SEE'.
AND WHEN THEY HAD FOUND OUT THEY SAID,
   'FIVE, AND TWO FISH'."
                MARK 6: 35-38

JESUS' STUDENTS, WHO FOR LACK OF
   AN **INNER SENSE OF ABUNDANCE**,
   HAVE A **SPIRITUALITY OF SCARCITY**.
THEY ARE IN A LATHER ABOUT HAVING SUPPER,
   AND THERE ***NOT BEING ENOUGH*** FOOD.
"SO GET RID OF THIS MOB, JESUS...
   SO WE CAN EAT WHAT WE HAVE!"
JESUS CHALLENGES THEIR IMPOVERISHED SPIRITUALITY
   AND ITS GRASPING EGO-CENTRISM SAYING,
     "**YOU** GIVE THEM SOMETHING TO EAT!"

THEY ARE ON THE EDGE OF THE ROOF NOW.
THERE IS NOTHING **INSIDE OR OUTSIDE TO GIVE**.

 "ARE WE TO GO AND BUY ALMOST A YEARS WAGES OF
   BREAD AND **GIVE IT TO THEM** TO EAT?"

THEIR VISION AND SPIRITUALITY IS CONTAINED
   IN THAT OUTCRY.
   IT'S US vs. THEM! IT'S SURVIVAL.
   THERE'S **NOT ENOUGH**!!!!
AND WE REALLY DON'T CARE ABOUT THEM.
THEY ARE **NOT MY NEW FAMILY**!

"THEN HE ORDERED THEM TO GET ALL THE PEOPLE TO SIT
   DOWN IN GROUPS ON THE GREEN GRASS,
   AND THEY SAT DOWN ON THE GROUND IN SQUARES
   OF HUNDREDS AND FIFTIES.
THEN HE TOOK THE FIVE LOAVES AND THE TWO FISH,
   RAISED HIS EYES TO HEAVEN AND SAID THE BLESSING;
   THEN HE BROKE THE LOAVES AND BEGAN HANDING THEM
   TO HIS DISCIPLES TO DISTRIBUTE AMONG THE PEOPLE.
HE ALSO SHARED OUT THE TWO FISH AMONG THEM ALL.
THEY ALL ATE AS MUCH AS THEY WANTED.
THEY COLLECTED TWELVE BASKETFULS OF SCRAPS
   OF BREAD AND PIECES OF FISH. THOSE WHO HAD EATEN
   THE LOAVES NUMBERED 5000 MEN."   MARK 6: 39-44

JESUS GETS THEM TO GO ***INTO THIS CROWD***
   AND CREATE COMMUNITIES OF 50 AND 100'S.
   THEY HAD TO ***"SEE"*** THESE PEOPLE
   WHO WERE HUNGRY LIKE THEY WERE.
   (THESE PEOPLE HAD BECOME LIKE THEIR **"SHADOW"**.)
     (THE 3RD PRACTICE).

THEN JESUS TAKES **"THEIR"** BREAD AND DRIED FISH
    AND LIFTS THEM UP. THEY MUST GET THIS!
    ALL FOOD IS FROM GOD! NO ONE OWNS IT.

IT'S GOD'S FOOD AND IT IS FOR EVERYONE.
    IT'S LIKE A "BREATH".
    IT'S FROM GOD AND IT GIVES LIFE AND WE **ALL** NEED IT.

JESUS BLESSES IT AND BREAKS
    GOD'S BREAD & FISH.
    HE GIVES IT TO THE DISCIPLES,
    SO THEY HAVE
        TO SHARE
    "THEIR" FOOD WITH
    "THOSE" PEOPLE.

WELL, WE DON'T KNOW WHAT HAPPENED,
    BUT I THINK THEY CREATED AN ENERGY FIELD
    THAT SWEPT THROUGH THIS CROWD.
    THE PEOPLE SEE THE DISCIPLES GIVING "THEIR"
    OWN FOOD TO THEM,
    AND GET **CAUGHT UP IN THE SPIRIT**.
    THEY BREAK OUT "THEIR OWN" STASH OF FOOD
    THEY HAD BEEN CLUTCHING ONTO.
    THEY BEGIN TO SHARE "THEIR" FOOD WITH
    THEIR NEIGHBOR NEXT TO THEM,
    AND SOON THE LID HAS BLOWN OFF,
    AND THERE IS FOOD GOING EVERYWHERE.
    EVEN THE HARDEST OF HEART FIND IT IRRESISTIBLE
    AND RELEASE THEIR GRIP ON "THEIR" BREAD.

THIS IS THE **SPIRIT- MOVEMENT** THAT
    TRANSFORMS A CROWD INTO A "FAMILY".
SURE, IT WAS GOD'S FOOD
    AND THEY WERE ALL CHILDREN OF GOD,
    BUT FOR ONCE
    THEY **KNEW** IT.

THERE WAS SO MUCH FOOD LEFT OVER THAT THE
    SPIRITUALITY OF SCARCITY WAS SHATTERED.
    AT LEAST IT WAS THAT DAY...
    THE DAY EVERYONE GOT TO
    SEE WHAT THE REIGN OF GOD
    LOOKED, FELT, AND
        TASTED LIKE.

THE SPIRIT-MOVEMENT: AN ALTAR FOR OUR EGO

THE SPIRITUALITY OF JESUS CHALLENGES US TO FIND AN ALTAR UPON WHICH TO OFFER OUR EGO. AND WE SEE THIS AS A PROCESS, OR SERIES OF ALTARS, WHICH ARE BEFORE US, AS THEY WERE BEFORE JESUS:

A) ALTAR OF EGO

```
        EGO
/-----------------------------\
   ||    EGO      ||
```

WE BEGIN HERE. EVERYTHING SERVES MY DESIRE. IT'S ALL ABOUT **ME** (EGO)!
"YOU ARE THINKING AS HUMANS DO, NOT AS GOD THINKS!" (JESUS TO PETER)

B) ALTAR OF RELIGION

```
        EGO
/-----------------------------\
   ||  RELIGION   ||
```

EGO IS TAMED HERE TO **SERVE ONE'S RELIGION**. IMPORTANT STEP TO LARGER REALITY AND FOUNDATION. MORE THAN "ME", A "WE" WITH PRACTICES, BELIEFS, ETHIC, COMMUNITY...

C) ALTAR OF SPIRIT

```
        EGO
/-----------------------------\
   ||   SPIRIT    ||
```

HERE EGO **SERVES THE SPIRIT (RUACH) OF GOD**. IT BLOWS WHERE IT WILL. JESUS WAS LURED, LED, DRIVEN, DRAWN, & CALLED BY "RUACH". WHEN CONFLICTED, SPIRIT TRUMPED RELIGION. SPIRIT BROUGHT FREEDOM, JOY, AND TROUBLE.

D) COMMUNAL ALTAR OF SPIRIT

```
EGO EGO EGO EGO
/-----------------------------\
   ||   SPIRIT    ||
```

LAYING OUR EGO ON THE **ALTAR OF SPIRIT TOGETHER**! A COMMUNITY MOVING WITH THE SPIRIT. THIS WAS JESUS' VISION: THE REIGN OF GOD BREAKING INTO THE WORLD! LITTLE EGOS CREATE A **UNITY** AND THEN A **COMMUNITY** THAT CAN IGNITE, EXCITE, EVEN TRANSFORM WORLD BY COMPASSION, SERVANTHOOD, CREATIVITY... THIS IS AN EXCITING SPIRIT- MOVEMENT.
WHERE WILL THE SPIRIT TAKE US?

3) NOT MY PARTY!

IN THE **PARABLE OF THE LOST SON(S)**: LUKE 15:11-32,
   JESUS FOCUSES ON THE OLDER BROTHER
   WHO IS LOST AS WELL.
   HE WAS RESENTFUL OF THE PARTY GOING ON FOR
   HIS BROTHER WHEN HE RETURNED FROM HIS WANTON &
   WASTEFUL JOURNEY ON THE FATHER'S DIME
   (NO ONE **OWES** YOU AN INHERITANCE!).

"NOW THE ELDER SON WAS OUT IN THE FIELDS, AND ON HIS WAY BACK,
AS HE DREW NEAR THE HOUSE, HE COULD HEAR MUSIC AND DANCING.
CALLING ONE OF THE SERVANTS, HE ASKED WHAT IT WAS ALL ABOUT.
THE SERVANT TOLD HIM,
   'YOUR BROTHER HAS COME, AND YOUR FATHER HAS KILLED
   THE CALF WE HAD BEEN FATTENING
   BECAUSE HE HAS GOT HIM BACK SAFE AND SOUND'.
HE WAS ANGRY THEN AND REFUSED TO GO IN,
AND HIS FATHER CAME OUT AND BEGAN TO URGE HIM TO COME IN; BUT
HE RETORTED TO HIS FATHER,
   'ALL THESE YEARS I HAVE SLAVED FOR YOU AND
   NEVER ONCE DISOBEYING ANY ORDERS OF YOURS,
   YET YOU NEVER OFFERED ME SO MUCH AS A KID
   FOR ME TO CELEBRATE WITH MY FRIENDS.
   BUT, FOR THIS SON OF YOURS, WHEN HE COMES BACK
   AFTER SWALLOWING UP YOUR PROPERTY —
   HE AND HIS LOOSE WOMEN— YOU KILL THE CALF
   WE HAD BEEN FATTENING.'"   LK. 15: 25 F.

THIS IS WHAT ONE'S SOUL LOOKS LIKE
   WITHOUT THE 2ND PRACTICE, AN X-RAY IMAGE.
THERE IS NO SPRING INSIDE,
      NO MUSIC INSIDE,
      NO DANCING INSIDE,
      NO FEAST INSIDE, NO LOVE INSIDE...
      JUST A GREAT EMPTINESS AND RESENTMENT.

THIS MAN/BOY CAN'T COME TO ANYONE'S PARTY
      BECAUSE **HE HAS NO PARTY INSIDE**.
      SO IF I CAN'T HAVE A PARTY,
      THEN NO ONE SHOULD HAVE ONE.

WITHOUT THE 2ND PRACTICE,
    WE ARE ALL OUT IN THE FIELD
    LISTENING TO THE MUSIC, HATING IT
    AND EVERYONE THERE BECAUSE
    THERE IS NO MUSIC IN US.
    FROM THIS DEPRIVATION COMES THE RESENTMENT,
    THE BITTERNESS, AND THE WITHHOLDING.
IF WE DO NOT **WADE INTO THE 2ND PRACTICE**
    AND **FACE UP TO THE 3RD PRACTICE**,
    THEN OUR INNER LIFE FEELS CHAOTIC,
    AND WE HAVE TO FIND A DISTRACTION.

JESUS EXPOSES US HERE IN THE STORY.
    WE HAVE TO TAKE RESPONSIBILITY
    FOR THE HEALING OF OUR HEART
    AND LET THE INNER MUSICIANS PLAY.
    OR WE'LL MAKE SURE THERE WILL BE
    NO PARTIES FOR ANYONE...
    AND **NO SPIRITUAL COMMUNITY**!

4) STILL ROOM AT THE TABLE

JESUS TELLS A STORY ABOUT A GREAT DINNER:

"THERE WAS A MAN WHO GAVE A GREAT BANQUET,
 AND HE INVITED A LARGE NUMBER OF PEOPLE.
WHEN THE TIME FOR THE BANQUET CAME, HE SENT HIS
SERVANT TO SAY TO THOSE WHO HAD BEEN INVITED,
   'COME ALONG: EVERYTHING IS READY NOW.'
BUT ALL ALIKE STARTED TO MAKE EXCUSES. THE FIRST SAID,
   'I HAVE BOUGHT A PIECE OF LAND AND MUST GO AND SEE
    IT. PLEASE ACCEPT MY APOLOGIES.'   ANOTHER SAID,
   'I HAVE BOUGHT FIVE YOKE OF OXEN AND AM ON MY WAY TO TRY
    THEM OUT. PLEASE ACCEPT MY APOLOGIES.'
YET ANOTHER SAID,
   'I HAVE JUST GOT MARRIED AND SO AM UNABLE TO COME.'

THE SERVANT RETURNED AND REPORTED THIS TO HIS MASTER. THEN
THE HOUSEHOLDER, IN A RAGE,
SAID TO HIS SERVANT,
   'GO OUT QUICKLY INTO THE STREETS AND ALLEYS OF THE
    TOWN AND BRING IN HERE THE POOR, THE CRIPPLED,
    THE BLIND AND THE LAME.'
'SIR', SAID THE SERVANT, 'YOUR ORDERS HAVE BEEN CARRIED OUT AND
THERE IS STILL ROOM.'

THEN THE MASTER SAID TO HIS SERVANT,
  'GO TO THE OPEN ROADS AND THE HEDGEROWS AND PRESS
  PEOPLE TO COME IN , TO MAKE SURE MY HOUSE IS FULL...'"
                                        LUKE 14:16-23

THE GREAT DINNER IS JESUS' METAPHOR FOR THE
  REIGN OF GOD IN THIS STORY,
    BUT ALSO A REAL TIME EVENT AT **HIS** DINNER TABLE.
        (THE 1ST PROTOTYPE: THE TABLE OF JESUS)
IT ALSO DRAMATIZES THE 2ND PRACTICE (DIVINE GRACE):
    FREE FOOD, GREAT MUSIC & DANCE & PEOPLE,
    AND THE PRESENCE OF THE GREAT HOST.

BUT EVERYBODY IS BUSY AND MAKE EXCUSES.
    THEY SOUND LIKE **ME**.
    "I'VE GOT STUFF TO DO... I HAVE TO CATCH UP AT HOME".

BUT THE HOST IS REALLY UPSET. AFTER ALL,
    THIS IS THE WAY TO CREATE SPIRITUAL COMMUNITY.
    THERE IS **DIVINE PASSION HERE**
    FOR THE HEALING OF THE WORLD.
    WE ARE BEING **CALLED TO THE TABLE**.

THE ANGER OF THE MASTER IS A MEASURE
    OF THE INTENSITY OF THE DESIRE.
ON A SMALL SCALE I KNOW HOW MUCH IT MEANS TO ME
    WHEN MY OWN CHILDREN COME HOME FOR
    A GREAT CELEBRATION.
    AND SO THE EXCUSES HURT AND DISAPPOINT.

THE INVITATION GOES OUT AGAIN,
    NOW TO THE BROKEN ONES,
    THE VULNERABLE, THE POOR,
    AND THEY ARE COMING IN.
SO NOW WE HAVE A **GREAT DIVERSITY OF HUMANITY**,
    LIKE THE WORLD, A REAL TAPESTRY.
WE'RE GOING TO MEET PEOPLE WE DON'T RUN WITH,
    IF WE GO, THAT IS.

AND THERE IS **STILL ROOM**!
    THE HOST WANTS HIS HOUSE FILLED.
    THEY'RE GOING EVERYWHERE NOW: OUTSIDE THE GATE,
    OUTSIDE THE FAITH, OUTSIDE OUR BOUNDARIES,
    OUR COMFORT ZONE... THIS IS OUT OF CONTROL!
    WHO ARE THESE PEOPLE?

5) RECONCILIATION

"IF YOU BRING YOUR GIFT TO THE ALTAR,
   AND THERE REMEMBER THAT YOUR BROTHER/SISTER
   HAS SOMETHING AGAINST YOU,
   LEAVE YOUR OFFERING THERE BEFORE THE ALTAR,
   GO AND BE RECONCILED (GREEK: "DIALLASSO")
   WITH THEM FIRST AND THEN COME BACK
   AND PRESENT YOUR OFFERING."   MATT. 5:23 F.

"DIALLASSO" = "DIA" (THROUGH/CROSS) +
                "-ALLOS" (THE OTHER)
IT MEANS TO CROSS THE BOUNDARIES/WALL
   SEPARATING YOU FROM "THE OTHER".
THIS TRANSFORMS **YOU**, THE **OTHER**, AND THE **BOUNDARY**.
   THIS IS RECONCILIATION.

"WHEN EVENING CAME, JESUS SAID,
'LET US 'CROSS OVER' (DIALLASSO) TO THE OTHER SIDE.'"
                                MARK 4:35

THEY LIVED ON THE JEWISH SIDE OF THE GALILEAN LAKE,
   THE GENTILES LIVED ON THE **OTHER** SIDE.
JESUS CROSSED OVER TO THE "HATED" GENTILES,
   TO THE "UNCLEAN" PLACE.
   AND HE BROUGHT THE DISCIPLES.
   IT WAS STRANGE OVER THERE,
   BUT IT WAS TO BE THE WAY THEY WERE TO LIVE.
   IT WAS A PATH OF RECONCILIATION.
   IT COULD TRANSFORM EVERYTHING.
"BUT A SAMARITAN TRAVELER WHO CAME ON HIM WAS MOVED WITH
COMPASSION WHEN HE SAW HIM.
HE WENT UP TO HIM...   LK. 10:33

THE SAMARITAN HAD
   A WELL OF GRACE IN HIM (**2ND PRACTICE**) AND HAD
   FACED HIS OWN WOUNDEDNESS (**3RD PRACTICE**),
   SO HE COULD **SEE** THE MAN
   AND HAVE COMPASSION (**4TH PRACTICE**).
HE WAS ABLE TO "CROSS OVER" TO THE OTHER SIDE OF THE ROAD AND
BROTHER THE STRANGER.
WHEN HE WAS DONE, THEY HAD BECOME DIFFERENT,
   SAMARITAN & JEW STILL, BUT RECONCILED NOW,
   SPIRITUAL COMMUNITY EVEN (**5TH PRACTICE**).

THIS IS A GREAT STORY WITH THE POWER
    TO TRANSFORM OUR HEART AND OUR WORLD.
    IT'S OUTRAGEOUS AND DARING.
    BUT IT'S ALSO AT THE HEART OF **WHO WE REALLY ARE**!

BUT THERE IS SO MUCH RESISTANCE TO THIS,
    EVEN IN THE CHURCH OF JESUS.
PEOPLE CONTINUE TO ASK AS LONG AGO THE
    RELIGIOUS LEADERS COMPLAINED:
  *"WHY DO DO YOU EAT & DRINK WITH HERETICS,
  CRIMINALS, AND LOSERS?"*   (CF. LK.5:30)

6) CELEBRATION

*"FOR JOHN CAME, NEITHER EATING NOR DRINKING,
AND THEY SAY, 'HE IS POSSESSED'.
THE SON OF MAN CAME, EATING & DRINKING, AND THEY SAY,
'LOOK, A GLUTTON & A DRUNKARD, A FRIEND OF
TAX COLLECTORS & SINNERS.'"*   MATTHEW 11:18F.

THE CONTRAST COULDN'T BE MORE STARK BETWEEN
    THESE TWO SPIRITUAL MOVEMENTS.
JOHN'S WAS INTENSE, SERIOUS, AND ASCETIC (SELF-
    DENYING/AUSTERE/LIFE-STYLE OF A MONK).
THEY WERE CRITICIZED FOR BEING **TOO STRICT & SOBER**.

IN CONTRAST, JESUS & HIS DISCIPLES SEEM TO BE ALWAYS
    "**AT THE TABLE**", LAUGHING, AND HAVING SEEMINGLY
    "TOO MUCH WINE".
    THEY WERE "HOMELESS" TRAVELERS
    WHO SLEPT IN THE PARKS WITH "QUESTIONABLE" WOMEN,
    AND AN ODD MIX OF MALE REJECTS & LOSERS.
    AND THEY ALL APPEARED TO BE
    WAY TOO HAPPY
    TO BE "RELIGIOUS".
    YOU CAN HEAR THE CRITICS NOW.

THIS IS A REAL WINDOW INTO THE "SPIRITUAL COMMUNITY"
    OF JESUS. IT IS CONSISTENT WITH JESUS' IMAGE OF THE
    REIGN OF GOD AS A WEDDING FEAST.
    THIS IS A CELEBRATION!
    THERE IS A WEDDING TO CELEBRATE.
    JESUS HAS FALLEN IN LOVE WITH THE DIVINE.
    AND NOW ***SO HAVE WE***! WE'RE **IN** THIS WEDDING!

WE ARE BETROTHED TO THE DIVINE BELOVED.
    THE SEASON OF FEAR & JUDGMENT IS OVER.
    IT IS THE SEASON OF FORGIVENESS, AND LOVE.

WHEN YOU FEEL THIS, THERE IS JOY,
    AND YOU WANT TO BEHOLD THIS DAY,
    AND YOU WANT TO CELEBRATE,
    AND YOU WANT TO SHARE IT,
    AND YOU DON'T WANT IT TO EVER END.

THIS IS WHAT THIS SPIRITUAL COMMUNITY IS LIKE,
    IN SPITE OF ALL THE CRITICS.

PRACTICAL MOVES TOWARD SPIRITUAL COMMUNITY:

HAVE A DINNER:
    INVITE PEOPLE YOU WOULDN'T NORMALLY EAT WITH.
    EVERYBODY LOVES TO EAT.

START A STUDY GROUP:
    HAVE OPEN INVITATION, EXTEND IT PERSONALLY.
    PEOPLE ARE ALSO HUNGRY FOR REAL CONVERSATION.

GET A SPIRITUAL FRIEND OR TWO:
    HAVE A REGULAR LUNCH TOGETHER.
    PEOPLE ARE HUNGRY FOR FOOD & REAL RELATIONSHIP.

WHY "SPIRITUAL COMMUNITY" MATTERS.

A VERY BRIGHT & CREATIVE WOMAN SPOKE TO A GROUP ABOUT WHAT THIS REALLY MEANS. I ASKED HER TO WRITE THIS TO THE WHOLE CONGREGATION, SINCE IT WAS ABOUT THEM. DEBORAH WROTE:

"I'VE BEEN LOST ALL MY LIFE, MOVING 50 TIMES IN 45 YEARS.

THEN, 14 YEARS AGO, MY HUSBAND AND I FOUND THIS PLACE,
*   THIS BROKEN LAND.*
*   WE HAVE BUILT A HOME HERE AND , EACH YEAR,*
*   WE HAVE HEALED THE LAND*
*   A LITTLE AT A TIME, STEP BY STEP.*

BUT, WE HAVE BEEN WITHOUT COMMUNITY, WITHOUT THE
*   SUPPORT AND ACCEPTANCE THAT COMES WITH COMMUNITY.*
*   DURING THESE 14 YEARS, I HAVE LOST ALL FOUR OF MY FAMILY*
*   OF ORIGIN, AND GAINED TWO LOST, BROKEN CHILDREN TO HEAL.*
*   IT HAS BEEN DIFFICULT.*

THEN, ABOUT A YEAR AGO,
*   I BEGAN ATTENDING TUESDAY MORNING DISCUSSIONS:*
*   A GROUP STUDYING BOOKS ABOUT THE JOURNEY WE ARE ALL ON.*

THIS WEEK I REALIZED I AM NO LONGER LOST.
*   I HAVE BEEN FOUND BY A COMMUNITY THAT LOVES & ACCEPTS ME,*
*   WHETHER I AM BUBBLING OVER WITH JOY,*
*   OR LOST IN SADNESS AND CONFUSION.*
*   THIS FAMILY WHERE I NOW BELONG IS EMMANUEL.*

AND IT HAS CHANGED ME.
*   I AM GENTLER WITH MY CRITICISM AND SLOWER TO ANGER.*
*   MOST WONDERFULLY, I HAVE MOMENTS OF*
*   ABSOLUTE PEACE AND CONTENTMENT.*

I AM BEING HEALED. THANK YOU."

THE 6TH PRACTICE: EMBRACING THE CALL

"It is 1991 and my colleague has retired.
   I must resign and the congregation must call a pastor.
   I don't know if I can do this alone or want to,
   or if the congregation even wants me to stay...?

I have a dream:
   'There is a strong looking man who appears to be in a
   coma and others around are giving up on him.
   I push my way in and stand him upright,
   looking in his blank eyes, calling him intensely
   back to life. He comes to life slowly, saying he has
   one thing left to do...there is a sense of confidence in the
   room that (he/I) can do this...'

I have another dream:
   'I am to catch a train and I come to a river and the train
   is about to leave on the other side of the river.
   I feel it is impossible, about to give up, and just then,
   a folding bridge begins to unfold from the other side of
   the river coming toward me and lands just before me.
   I can now cross the river.'

I awaken from both dreams feeling that I am being urged
   to awaken to life and this work before me and
   trust wholly in the Divine Grace to come..."

THE CALL OF JESUS

MARK 1: 9-11.
   "JESUS WAS BAPTIZED IN THE JORDAN BY JOHN. AND AT
   ONCE, AS HE WAS COMING UP OUT OF THE WATER, HE SAW
   THE HEAVENS TORN APART AND THE SPIRIT, LIKE A DOVE,
   DESCENDING ON HIM. AND A VOICE CAME FROM HEAVEN,
   'YOU ARE MY SON, THE BELOVED...'"
   THE CALL BEGINS WITH AN
   IMMERSION IN DIVINE GRACE (2ND PRACTICE).

MARK 1:12-13.
   "...THE SPIRIT DROVE HIM INTO THE DESERT AND HE
   REMAINED THERE FOR 40 DAYS, AND PUT TO THE TEST BY
   THE ADVERSARY. HE WAS WITH THE WILD ANIMALS,
   AND THE ANGELS..."

IT CONTINUES WITH A WRESTLING AND DISCERNING
PROCESS (3RD PRACTICE)
THE DESERT STRUGGLE ENDS WITH ANOTHER
IMMERSION IN GRACE, THIS TIME IN THE DESERT
WITH WILD ANIMALS & ANGELS.

MARK 1:14-15.
   "AFTER JOHN HAD BEEN ARRESTED,
   JESUS WENT INTO GALILEE.
   THERE HE PROCLAIMED THE GOSPEL FROM GOD..."
   ALL OF THIS "CALL PROCESS" SEEMS TO BE HAPPENING
   INSIDE JESUS- A GREAT INWARD STRUGGLE TO DISCERN
   WHAT *HIS* PART IN THE GREAT WORK OF GOD WOULD BE.
   BUT THEN THE STRUGGLE IN THE WORLD IMPACTS HIM,
   AND HE **LETS** IT. SOMETIMES THERE IS AN EVENT
   THAT   TRIGGERS US — THAT SOUNDS AN ALARM.
   THIS IS THE TIME: "*KAIROS*"!
   NOW IS THE TIME TO COME FORTH
        AND BEGIN THE WORK.
   JOHN, HIS FRIEND AND MENTOR,
   WAS ALREADY OUT THERE DOING **HIS** CALL.
   AND WHEN JOHN WAS ARRESTED, THEY ALL KNEW HE
   WOULD BE **SILENCED PERMANENTLY**, ALL THE PROPHETS
   OF GOD WERE. THAT WAS HOW YOU OFTEN KNEW A **REAL**
   ONE. THIS WAS A GREAT LOSS FOR JESUS.
   WAS IT HIS GRIEF... HIS ANGER THAT
   CAUSED JESUS TO STEP **UP** WHEN JOHN WENT **DOWN**?
   THERE IS ENERGY IN THAT GRIEF—ANGER.
   IT CAN EAT US UP **OR** BECOME THE ROCKET FUEL
   FOR A CALL — A CREATIVE WORK.
   SO JESUS IS LAUNCHED INTO HIS CALL BY AN ACT OF
   INJUSTICE AND THE IMPENDING TORTURE OF JOHN.
   JESUS FOUND HIS VOICE WHEN JOHN WAS SILENCED.

MARK 1:15
   "...THE TIME IS FULFILLED AND
   THE REIGN OF GOD IS CLOSE AT HAND.
   BE TRANSFORMED & AND TRUST THE GOOD NEWS."
   THIS IS THE EXTREMELY POWERFUL MESSAGE OF JESUS
   HEWED BY SOLITUDE & GRIEF & LONGING & PRAYER.
   SUCCINCT LIKE A SEED... OF SACRED FIRE.

MARK 1: 16-18.
   "AS HE WAS WALKING ALONG BY THE LAKE OF GALILEE HE
   SAW SIMON AND SIMON'S BROTHER ANDREW CASTING A
   NET IN THE LAKE — FOR THEY WERE FISHERMEN.

*AND JESUS SAID TO THEM, 'COME AFTER ME AND
I WILL MAKE YOU INTO FISHERS OF PEOPLE.'
AND AT ONCE THEY LEFT THEIR NETS AND FOLLOWED HIM."*

THEN HE GATHERED TOGETHER A SPIRITUAL COMMUNITY
(5TH PRACTICE). THE CALL MAY BE LONELY AT TIMES,
BUT HE WAS NOT TO BE ALONE.
HIS GREAT COMPASSION ALSO DREW THE SICK AND
SUFFERING TO HIM.
SO HE FOUND HIMSELF IN A HEALING MINISTRY TOO,
BUT IT WAS NOT THE FOCUS OF HIS CALL.

MARK 1:32 F.
*"THAT EVENING , AFTER SUNSET, THEY BROUGHT TO HIM
ALL WHO WERE SICK AND THOSE WHO WERE POSSESSED
BY DEVILS. THE WHOLE TOWN CAME CROWDING
ROUND THE DOOR...
IN THE MORNING, LONG BEFORE DAWN, HE GOT UP AND
LEFT THE HOUSE AND WENT OFF TO A LONELY PLACE AND
PRAYED THERE. SIMON AND HIS COMPANIONS SET OUT IN
SEARCH OF HIM, AND WHEN THEY FOUND HIM THEY SAID,
'EVERYBODY IS LOOKING FOR YOU.'   HE ANSWERED,
'LET US GO ELSEWHERE, TO THE NEIGHBORING
COUNTRY TOWNS, SO THAT I CAN PROCLAIM THE MESSAGE
THERE TOO, BECAUSE THAT IS WHY I CAME..."*

WHEN WE COME OUT INTO THE PUBLIC, WE CAN GET
INVOLVED IN **MANY** THINGS BECAUSE WE HAVE
ENTHUSIASM, AND THERE IS SO MUCH NEED.
SO IT IS ESSENTIAL TO RETURN TO THE FOCUS OF OUR CALL.

NOTICE HOW JESUS RETURNS TO THE PRACTICES OF THE
INNER LIFE TO FIND DIRECTION IN THE MIDST OF ALL THESE
AFFLICTED PEOPLE AND ANXIOUS DISCIPLES.
IT IS THIS KIND OF SOLITUDE & PRAYER THAT
ENERGIZES AND REFOCUSES US.

IF JESUS RESPONDED TO EVERY NEED,
HE COULD EASILY LOSE HIMSELF. HE COUNSELS US TO
LOSE OUR "FALSE SELVES" IN OUR JOURNEY WITH GOD,
THEREFORE FINDING OUR "REAL SELF".

IF WE LOSE "OURSELVES" JUST TRYING TO MEET
OTHER'S EXPECTATIONS, EVEN DEMANDS,
WE JUST END UP LOST AND EMPTY.

HOW DO WE *"DISCERN"* OUR "CALL"?

OUR CALL OR VOCATION IS WRITTEN DEEP IN OUR SOUL.
VOCATION COMES FROM THE WORD "VOCARE" WHICH
MEANS "TO CALL". VOCATION IS NOT A GOAL THAT
I PURSUE, BUT A CALLING THAT I "HEAR".

PARKER PALMER IN *"LET YOUR LIFE SPEAK"* [12], SAYS THAT
BEFORE I CAN TELL MY LIFE WHAT I WANT TO DO WITH IT,
I MUST LISTEN TO MY LIFE TELLING ME WHO I AM.
I WOULD SAY THAT THE CALL IS **NOT**:
...A DESIRE TO MEET OTHERS' (PARENTS, FRIENDS)
    EXPECTATIONS
...THE URGENCY OF MY EGO TO SUCCEED
...EVEN THE HONORABLE URGE TO BE RESPONSIBLE

A CALLING COMES FROM A DEEPER / TRUER PLACE IN ME
THAT EXPRESSES MY REAL IDENTITY AND SELF. IT COMES
OUT OF OUR INNER LIFE — OUR DREAMING AND LONGING
AND PRAYING, AS IT DID WITH JESUS.
AND THEN IT FUMBLES OUTWARD IN DARING, RISKY FORAYS
INTO THE WORK. WE DON'T KNOW WHERE IT GOES,
BUT IT GOES... **WE REFINE, RETUNE UNTIL OUR WORK IN
THE WORLD IS IN HARMONY WITH THE VISION INSIDE.
WE HAVE TO BE WILLING TO ADVENTURE... AND FAIL.**

TO GET PERSONAL.... I WENT OFF TO GRADUATE SCHOOL IN
NUCLEAR CHEMISTRY AT IOWA STATE UNIVERSITY. I THOUGHT
I KNEW MY CALLING, THOUGH I WAS AN ATHEIST. WHILE
THERE, I GOT DIS-ILLUSIONED, LOST MY HEART FOR IT,
LOST MY BEST FRIEND, WAS LOSING MY HEALTH, AND
EVENTUALLY DROPPED OUT, AND WENT HOME TO CHICAGO.
IT WAS A FAILURE IN EVERY WAY EXCEPT THAT IN THE
BREAKING APART OF MY LIFE,
I HAD AN EXPERIENCE OF GOD. I HEARD A VOICE
ADDRESSING ME: "RENEW THE CHURCH" AND HAD A
VISION OF "CROSSES". ACTUALLY I HATED CHURCHES AND
HAD NO IDEA HOW TO RENEW EVEN MYSELF.
**BUT I DISCOVERED GOD WAS MORE INTERESTED IN ME
THAN I WAS.**

I ALSO DISCOVERED AFTER ASST. TEACHING FRESHMAN
CHEMISTRY THAT I LIKED TEACHING, AND I BEGAN TO
REALLY LIKE PEOPLE.

OUT OF THE ASHES,
   I EVENTUALLY WENT INTO THEOLOGICAL SEMINARY.

*OVER AND OVER IN MY LIFE I HAVE FOLLOWED SOME **INSTINCT** TO DO SOMETHING, AND EXPERIENCED SOME SENSE OF **FAILURE, ONLY** TO FIND SOMETHING **VALUABLE** ABOUT MYSELF AND MY CALLING.*

IN 1969 I WENT OFF TO BE A HOSPITAL CHAPLAIN AT ELGIN STATE
   HOSPITAL, SO I COULD AVOID BEING IN A CHURCH. AS A
   HEALING INSTITUTION, IT WAS A FAILURE, AND I BECAME
   PART OF ITS FAILURE, AND I WAS TAKEN DOWN INTO THE
   DARKNESS WITH ALL THE LOST PATIENTS.

BUT I DID FIND THAT I WAS NOT FAR FROM MY CALLING.
   I FOUND MYSELF THERE IN THAT DARK PLACE AND I,
   LIKE THE PATIENTS, WAS LOST AND DIDN'T KNOW THE WAY
   TO BRING HEALING TO MYSELF OR TO THEM.

I HAD TO GO TO A CHURCH FOR 3 YEARS TO COMPLETE MY
   CLINICAL SUPERVISOR TRAINING. CONGREGATIONS ARE
   LIKE STATE HOSPITALS IN SOME WAYS, AND I FOUND IT TO
   BE A MICROCOSM OF THE WORLD AS WELL. IT FASCINATED
   AND CHALLENGED ME. I WAS A FAILURE, OF COURSE,
   BECAUSE **NOW IN MY NEW PROFESSIONAL STATUS**,
   I DIDN'T KNOW I NEEDED HEALING, OR, IF I DID,
   WHERE EVEN TO BEGIN.

EVENTUALLY, I HAD A BREAKDOWN/BREAKTHROUGH IN THE
   LATE 1970'S. THOUGH I WAS "SUCCESSFUL" AS A PASTOR,
   I HAD TO ADMIT THAT I WAS FAR FROM GOD...
   ....AND THAT I WAS LOST-- THE GREATEST FAILURE.

BUT THIS TIME I WAS SO DESPERATE, I WENT ALL OVER THE
   COUNTRY TO FIND HEALING AND FINALLY LEARN ABOUT THE
   SPIRITUAL JOURNEY.
   IN NO TIME A TEACHER/HEALER
   SHOWED UP IN UPPER NEW YORK,
   THEN ONE IN NEW MEXICO,
    A COMMUNITY IN WASHINGTON D.C.,
    A MOVEMENT IN MINNESOTA,
    AND IN CALIFORNIA...

I HAD HAD A CALLING,
   BUT THEN I BEGAN TO BE TRANSFORMED INTO
   SOMEONE WHO CAN "***EMBRACE THE CALL***".

RUMI SAYS:
> *"DRUNKS ARGUE AND GET INTO FIGHTS*
> *LOVERS ARE JUST AS BAD,*
> *THEY FALL IN A HOLE,*
> *BUT THEN DISCOVER SOMETHING SHINING THERE."*   [13]

THERE IS NO WAY TO BE ON THIS ADVENTURE WITHOUT
    VENTURING, AND WITHOUT
    FALLING INTO HOLES.
    BUT THEN SOMETHING "**SHINING**" APPEARS IN THE DARK.
    IT IS THE GIFT OF GOD, ***THE ENCOURAGEMENT***
      TO <u>STAY</u> ON THE JOURNEY
      AND <u>DISCOVER YOUR CALL,</u>
      AND <u>EMBRACE IT.</u>

"...WITH THEM AT TABLE WAS A LARGE GATHERING OF TAX
COLLECTORS AND OTHERS. THE PHARISEES AND THEIR
SCRIBES COMPLAINED TO HIS DISCIPLES AND SAID,
'WHY DO YOU EAT AND DRINK WITH TAX COLLECTORS
AND SINNERS?' JESUS SAID...
'IT IS NOT THOSE THAT ARE WELL WHO NEED THE DOCTOR,
BUT THE SICK. I HAVE COME TO CALL <u>NOT</u> THE UPRIGHT,
BUT THE FAILURES TO METANOIA (TRANSFORMATION).'"
                LK.5: 29F.

WE HAVE TRIED SO HARD TO AVOID "**FAILURE**",
    OR EVEN THE APPEARANCE OF IT,
    THAT WE HAVE NOT BEEN WILLING TO TAKE THE CHANCE,
    TO LEAVE THE HARBOR,
    TO DARE THE DREAM.

AND IRONICALLY THEN, IN OUR SAFE,
    PREDICTABLE, AND "SUCCESSFUL" LIVES,
    WE GET OBSESSED SO EASILY IN GAMBLING, INVESTING,
    SHOPPING, DRINKING, AND OTHER "***RISKY***" OBSESSIONS.
    AND DOESN'T EVERYTHING THAT TAKES US FARTHER FROM
    OUR "CALL", BECOME A ***RISK*** TO OUR VERY SOUL?

OBVIOUSLY, TO DISCERN ONE'S CALL IS TO **<u>LISTEN DEEPLY</u>**.
    THIS IS THE MEANING OF THE CORE OF THE JUDIASM OF
    JESUS. "SHEMA YISRAEL" IS HEBREW FOR
    "HEAR, O ISRAEL".
    "**<u>LISTEN</u>**................."

JESUS TELLS THEM TO PRAY IN A DARK CLOSET WHERE THEY CAN'T READ A PRAYER... A PLACE ONLY TO <u>LISTEN</u>.   MT.6:6

AND THEN AT THE END OF JESUS' LIFE,
   HE TAKES THEM UP A MOUNTAIN TO LEARN PRAYER,
   AND THERE THEY HEAR THE ONLY WORD THEY EVER HEAR
   FROM GOD DIRECTLY IN THE GOSPELS.
   AND THE VERB, THE CALL, THE PLEA FROM GOD WAS:
   (YOU GUESSED IT)
   "<u>LISTEN</u>..."   MARK 9: 7

HOW DO WE "*EMBRACE*" OUR CALL?

MY FAVORITE STORY OF "EMBRACING THE CALL" IS
   THE STORY OF MOSES FROM EXODUS 3:

"MOSES, LOOKING AFTER THE FLOCK...
   CAME TO HOREB, THE MOUNTAIN OF GOD.
THE ANGEL OF YHVH APPEARED TO HIM IN A FLAME BLAZING
   FROM THE MIDDLE OF A BUSH. MOSES LOOKED...
   THERE WAS THE BUSH BLAZING,
   BUT THE BUSH WAS NOT BEING BURNT UP.
MOSES SAID, 'I MUST GO ACROSS AND SEE THIS STRANGE
   SIGHT...' WHEN YHVH SAW HIM GOING ACROSS TO LOOK,
   GOD CALLED TO HIM FROM THE MIDDLE OF THE BUSH.
   'MOSES, MOSES!' HE SAID.
   'HERE I AM, HE ANSWERED.
   'COME NO NEARER,' HE SAID. 'TAKE OFF YOUR SANDALS,
   FOR <u>THE PLACE WHERE YOU ARE STANDING IS</u>
   <u>HOLY GROUND.   I AM THE GOD OF YOUR ANCESTORS</u>...
   THE GOD OF ABRAHAM, THE GOD OF ISAAC, AND THE GOD
   OF JACOB.' AT THIS MOSES COVERED HIS FACE,
   FOR HE WAS AFRAID TO LOOK AT GOD.
   'I HAVE INDEED SEEN THE MISERY OF MY PEOPLE IN EGYPT.
   <u>I HAVE HEARD THEM CRYING FOR HELP</u>...
   SO <u>NOW I AM SENDING YOU TO PHARAOH</u>,
   FOR YOU TO BRING MY PEOPLE... OUT OF EGYPT.'
MOSES SAID TO GOD, <u>'WHO AM I TO GO TO PHARAOH</u>
   AND BRING THE ISRAELITES OUT OF EGYPT?'
<u>'I SHALL BE WITH YOU</u>,' GOD SAID..."

"MOSES, MOSES!"
THE CALL BEGINS WITH HIS NAME. IT OFTEN DOES.
   IT SAYS, "I KNOW WHO YOU ARE—BETTER THAN YOU DO—
      WHO YOU <u>REALLY ARE</u>.

THIS IS THE TIME FOR
                  YOU TO BECOME **THAT. LISTEN!**"
THE GOOD PART HERE IS MOSES' CURIOSITY AND
       INTELLIGENCE.
       HE COULD MOVE AWAY. HE COMES **NEARER** –
       SO NEAR NOW THAT HE MUST REALIZE THAT HE IS
       ON **HOLY GROUND** AND MUST TAKE OFF HIS SANDALS.
IT BEGINS TO HIT HIM THAT HE HAS **ALWAYS** BEEN ON HOLY
    GROUND BUT NEVER KNEW **IT** BELONGED TO GOD—
    OR THAT **HE** BELONGED TOO—WHOEVER HE **REALLY** WAS.
    (WE DREAM SACRED DRAMAS OF OUR SOUL-LIFE
    90 MINUTES EVERY NIGHT, WE HAVE HEARD
    OUR NAME CALLED WITHIN OUR SILENCES.
    WE SEE AMAZING BEAUTY UNVEILED IN THE CREATION
    DAILY & NIGHTLY, YET WE HAVE TO BE JARRED *AWAKE*
    THAT WE ARE ON "**HOLY GROUND**")

"*I AM THE GOD OF YOUR ANCESTORS*".
    THIS GOD HAD ONLY BEEN A **STORY** HANDED DOWN FROM
    GRANDPARENTS. NOW GOD IS IN REAL TIME.

"*I AM SENDING YOU TO PHARAOH!*"
    MOSES RESPONDS, "WHO AM I TO GO TO PHARAOH...?"
    HIS FEARS & INADEQUACY ARE EXPOSED.
    HE HAS HEARD THIS VOICE (CALL) BEFORE AND
    HE HAS BEEN HIDING FROM IT AMONG THE SHEEP.
    BUT YOU CAN'T RUN AWAY FROM THE SOUL
    WHERE THE VOICE ACTUALLY RESIDES.
    AND YOU CAN'T RUN AWAY FROM THAT FIRE YOU WILL
    BADLY NEED LATER ON.
  MOSES THROWS UP PROTESTS TO CALL OFF GOD,
    AND GO BACK TO HIS ORDINARY LIFE
    (AND STAY OUT OF THE BIBLE AS WELL),
    EVEN IF IT MEANS HE WILL BE EMPTY & LOST.
    EMPTY & LOST IS BETTER THAN SCARED & POWER-FILLED.
    ISN'T IT??

"*I WILL BE WITH YOU!*"
THAT'S IT RIGHT THERE.
    THAT'S ALL WE EVER NEED TO KNOW.
THIS IS A JOINT VENTURE...
    A PARTNERSHIP WITH THE DIVINE.
THEREFORE, EVEN IF IT **APPEARS** TO FAIL,
    IT WILL BE DIVINELY/ SURPRISINGLY **CREATIVE**.
    GOD IS ALWAYS SURPRISING & CREATIVE,
    SO WE JUST HAVE TO **TRUST**.

AND WE HAVE ALL BEEN "DINGED"
   IN THE "TRUST" DEPARTMENT.
WE HAVE PLENTY OF REASONS **NOT** TO TRUST,
   BUT THIS IS **DIFFERENT.**

"I WILL BE WITH YOU" IS TO ENTER INTO
   THE GREATEST PARTNERSHIP WE COULD EVER HOPE FOR.
   IT WORKED FOR MOSES AND ALL THE PEOPLE INFLUENCED
   BY THIS GREAT BIBLICAL STORY.
   (MARTIN LUTHER KING JR. COMES TO MIND)
   WHO HAS NOT BEEN MOVED BY THIS ADVENTURE IN SPIRIT?

SO WHAT HAVE WE GOT TO *LOSE*—
   JUST SOME ILLUSIONS ABOUT OURSELVES,
   SOME EGO-CENTRICITY WE DON'T NEED,
   SOME PARALYZING FEAR TO LEAVE OUR HOUSE
      FOR OUR TRUE HOME,
   SOME FALSE & WEARY SELVES...
ONLY TO DISCOVER WHO WE **REALLY ARE**...

   "IF ONE IS AFRAID OF LOSING ANYTHING,
     THEY HAVE NOT LOOKED
     INTO THE FRIEND'S EYES."   [14]   HAFIZ

JESUS' CALL TO BE CREATIVE

"REMAIN IN ME, AS I IN YOU.
   AS A BRANCH CANNOT BEAR FRUIT ALL BY ITSELF,
   UNLESS IT REMAINS PART OF THE VINE,
   NEITHER CAN YOU UNLESS YOU REMAIN IN ME.
I AM THE VINE, YOU ARE THE BRANCHES.
   WHOEVER REMAINS IN ME, WITH ME IN THEM,
   BEARS FRUIT IN PLENTY;
   FOR CUT OFF FROM ME YOU CAN DO NOTHING...
I SHALL NO LONGER CALL YOU SERVANTS,
   BECAUSE A SERVANT DOES NOT KNOW
   THEIR MASTER'S BUSINESS.
I CALL YOU FRIENDS,
   BECAUSE I HAVE MADE KNOWN TO YOU
   EVERYTHING I HAVE LEARNT FROM ABBA.
YOU DID NOT CHOOSE ME,
   NO, I CHOSE YOU;
AND I COMMISSIONED YOU
   TO GO OUT AND TO BEAR FRUIT,
   FRUIT THAT WILL LAST..."   JOHN 15: 4-5,15-16

THE INNER LIFE & OUTER LIFE ARE EN-TWINED IN THIS IMAGE.
THE 1ST AND 2ND PRACTICES NOURISH THIS CONNECTION
   BETWEEN THE VINE & THE BRANCH.
    WE ARE ROOTED IN THE DIVINE. THIS IS OUR NATURE.
    WE ARE NURTURING OUR OWN NATURE.
    AND THEN WE BECOME FRUITFUL, THAT IS, CREATIVE.
    AND OUR CALL IS TO BE CREATIVE.

***"I APPOINTED YOU TO GO AND BEAR FRUIT —
   FRUIT THAT WILL LAST."***

IT WON'T BE THE SAME OLD TIRED THING THAT WE DO,
   FOR IT COMES FROM **INSIDE US**,
    ACTUALLY ***THROUGH US*** FROM THE DIVINE WELLSPRING,
      THE DI-***VINE***.

SO MAYBE THE BEST WAY TO DISCERN THE CALL IS
   TO "ABIDE IN THE VINE"
   AND LET IT MOVE IN AND THOUGH US.
IT HAS TO BE CREATIVE FOR IT COMES FROM THE CREATOR.
   AND IT WILL BEAR FRUIT, FOR WE ARE CONNECTED
   TO THE FRUITING ENERGY.
HOW IT HAPPENS IS A MYSTERY—
   ONE THAT TAKES US ONTO OUR KNEES.
WHAT A BLESSING TO BE PART
   OF SUCH A SACRED PROCESS!

TAKE AN APPLE INTO YOUR HAND —
   OR MY FAVORITE, A RASPBERRY.
   THAT IS THE SYMBOL, AND WHAT A DELICIOUS ONE,
   OF WHERE THIS IS ALL GOING.

THIS IS WHAT YOUR CALL WILL PRODUCE —
   APPLES & RASPBERRIES—WHAT JUICY BEAUTY,
   COLOR, FRAGRANCE, TASTE AND NUTRITION!
   THIS IS HEALING AND EMPOWERING TO THE WORLD.
   THIS IS A SIGN OF GRACE,
     OF HIDDEN DIVINE PRESENCE,
     FLOWERING & FRUITING AROUND US.

PRACTICAL STEPS FOR
DISCERNING THE CALL

KEEP A JOURNAL

MAKE AN INVESTMENT IN YOUR INWARD JOURNEY.
BUY A JOURNAL AND KEEP IT CLOSE.
WRITING CAN BE A WINDOW INTO THE SOUL.
WHY NOT TAKE A LOOK IN THE WINDOW?

TRACK YOUR DREAMS

WE DREAM 90 MINUTES NIGHTLY
   WITH IMAGES ON A LEVEL WITH VAN GOGH
   AND STORIES ON A PAR WITH SHAKESPEARE.
PUT A DREAM SECTION IN YOUR JOURNAL AND PUT DOWN
   WHATEVER YOU CAN RECALL THE **VERY FIRST THING**
   EVERY MORNING.
WHY NOT PAY ATTENTION TO THE GENIUS AT WORK
   IN YOUR BEDROOM EVERY NIGHT?

LET YOUR SOUL BE YOUR PILOT

EXPLORE WHAT YOU ARE DRAWN TO...
   WHAT YOU REALLY LOVE....
   WHERE YOUR PASSION IS... AND DARE TO INVESTIGATE,
   EVEN IF IT IS OUTSIDE YOUR COMFORT ZONE.
LET YOUR "CHILD" TAKE YOU TOWARD THEIR "DELIGHT".

TAKE A PILGRIMAGE

EVERY YEAR I GO SOMEWHERE AND STAY THERE
   UNTIL I "HEAR" WHAT GOD WANTS ME TO DO
   THAT YEAR, IF IT WOULD BE THE LAST YEAR OF MY LIFE.
SINCE I ALMOST DIED IN THE 1980'S,
   I THINK IT REALLY COULD BE.
YEARS AGO I HAD TO GO OUT ON MOUNTAINS IN
   SNOWSTORMS, OR OUT IN LAKE MICHIGAN
   AT NIGHT IN MY KAYAK, ETC.
NOW I CAN JUST GO TO A REMOTE PLACE, SETTLE DOWN,
   AND PRAY AND SING FOR DIRECTION.
AND IT ALWAYS COMES, SO I CAN GO HOME.
AND THAT IS WHAT I DO THAT YEAR.
AND THAT'S WHY I'M WRITING THIS.
PILGRIMAGE WORKS.
FIND A SACRED SPACE, HOWEVER HUMBLE IT MAY BE.

FIND A SPIRITUAL GUIDE

THERE ARE MENTORS AND ELDERS AROUND.
PRAY FOR THE RIGHT ONE. TEST DRIVE THEM.
IT IS SOMEONE WHO HAS MILES ON THEIR JOURNEY,
   CAN LISTEN, AND IS INTERESTED IN YOU.
DON'T BE PASSIVE OR SWALLOW ANYTHING WHOLE.
CHEW **EVERYTHING** AND DON'T GIVE AWAY ANY
   OF YOUR HARD- EARNED POWER TO DISCERN.
SEE THEM AS A COMPANION, NOT A GURU.
IF YOU FALL IN LOVE WITH THEM, THAT CAN BE GOOD.
JUST REMEMBER YOU ARE FALLING IN LOVE
   WITH THE DIVINE IN THEM.

PRACTICAL STEPS FOR
EMBRACING THE CALL

STOP RUNNING AWAY

TAKE A SERIOUS READ OF THE BOOK OF JONAH
IN THE BIBLE.
 I WAS DRAWN TO GET TOGETHER WITH THE
   LOCAL JEWISH RABBI AND THE MUSLIM IMAM.
 I TRIED TO GET SOMEONE ELSE TO DO IT INSTEAD OF ME.
   THAT MAN AGREED TO DO IT, BUT DID NOTHING.

 I TRIED TO IGNORE IT. TWO YEARS PASSED.
   IT DIDN'T GO AWAY.

THEN FINALLY I CALLED THEM MYSELF AND
   GOT TOGETHER WITH THEM FOR LUNCH.

AND OUT OF THIS LUNCH HAS COME THREE YEARS
   OF FRIENDSHIP AND "TRI-ALOGUES"
   WHERE WE GO AROUND TOGETHER
   TO THE CHRISTIAN CHURCH, THE MUSLIM MOSQUE,
   THE JEWISH TEMPLE, AND NOW SCHOOLS
   TO SPEAK AND ANSWER QUESTIONS
   ABOUT OUR TRADITIONS.
   WE HAVE ALL LEARNED SO MUCH,
    AND OUR FRIENDSHIP IS A REAL MODEL
    FOR A LARGER "SENSE OF FAMILY",
    A BROADER "SPIRITUAL COMMUNITY",
    AND A RICHER LIFE AS A CITY.
    (ONLY WHY DID IT TAKE ME SO LONG?)

WHEN IT IS A REAL CALLING,
     IT JUST DOESN'T GO AWAY.
     IT JUST GOES DEEPER INTO OUR CELLS AND HAUNTS US.
     IT CAN ALSO PRODUCE INDIGESTION.
     CHECK OUT YOUR INTESTINES.

WE ARE TO DIGEST THIS "WORD OF GOD" TO US,
     AS WELL AS THE FOOD GIVEN BY THE HAND OF GOD.
     BOTH THESE "FOODS" FUEL OUR REAL WORK/PLAY
     IN THE WORLD.

"HOW SWEET ARE YOUR WORDS TO MY MOUTH..."
                           PSALM 119: 103

SURRENDER

     IF I CAN GIVE UP RUNNING AWAY AND
         EMBRACE WHAT I KNOW I AM BEING CALLED TO,
         I HAVE SURRENDERED.

     THIS GIVES ME ENERGY, EMPOWERMENT,
         AND AN INNER PEACE,
         EVEN THOUGH THERE MAY BE CONFLICT ALL AROUND.

     WE CAN'T EXPLAIN THIS.

     WE HAVE TO TRUST THAT WHEN WE ENTER THIS CALL,
         WE ARE SOMEHOW IN GREATER HANDS.
         DESTINY IS AT WORK.

     THERE IS NOT NECESSARILY "SUCCESS",
         BUT IT WILL BE "CREATIVE",
         AND THERE WILL BE "BLESSING".

     JESUS ENCOUNTERS SO MUCH "FAILURE" IN HIS LIFE:
         THE HOSTILITY OF HIS RELIGIOUS LEADERS,
         REJECTION BY HIS HOME SYNAGOGUE,
         THE INABILITY OF HIS DISCIPLES TO GRASP HIS WORK,
             OR HIS HEART,
         AND THEN THE ABANDONMENTS, BETRAYALS...

     HE SEEMS TO HAVE TASTED ALL
         THE FLAVORS OF FAILURE,
         YET HERE WE ARE SIFTING THROUGH
         21 CENTURIES TO GET TO THE LUMINOUS GESTURES
         AND WORDS OF HIS AMAZING LIFE...

CHAPTER IV
"THE EMPOWERMENT"

1) LIFE-BREATH

"YHVH GOD SHAPED 'ADAM' (HUMAN)
FROM THE SOIL OF 'ADAMAH' (HUMIS)
AND BLEW THE BREATH (HEBREW: RUACH) OF LIFE
INTO 'ADAM'S' NOSTRILS,
AND 'ADAM' BECAME A LIVING BEING"

GENESIS 2:7

("RUACH" IS HEBREW FOR WIND/BREATH/SPIRIT)

WE BREATHE 10 TIMES A MINUTE
600 TIMES AN HOUR
14,400 TIMES A DAY
5 MILLION TIMES A YEAR

EACH BREATH IS GRACE...
AN UNREQUESTED GIFT OF THE BELOVED
WE LIVE IMMERSED IN THIS SEA OF GRACE

TAKE A BREATH!................

THIS BREATH TAKES US INTO THIS MOMENT...

IT RE-INACTS THE CREATION EXPERIENCE.

IT IS AN INTIMATE SPIRITUAL GIFT.

WE ARE "***BEING BREATHED***".
WE **DON'T BREATHE** –
THAT WOULD BE A CONSCIOUS ACT.
IF IT WERE STRICTLY UP TO ME,
I WOULD SURELY FORGET.
AND I WOULD NEVER BE ABLE TO SLEEP
OR EVEN REST.

RATHER WE ARE "***BREATHED***"
ALL DAY AND ALL NIGHT.
IT IS OUR NATURE TO CONTINUALLY RE-INACT GENESIS 2:7,
AND BE BREATHED INTO, OVER & OVER......

IS THAT WHY BECOMING CONSCIOUS OF OUR BREATH
TAKES US INTO SUCH
A GRACEFUL, CENTERED SPACE?

THE SCIENCE IS AMAZING, WHAT WITH THE OXYGEN ATOMS
   CONNECTING WITH RED BLOOD CELLS AND JOURNEYING
   WITHIN RIVERS AND BRINGING THIS RICH FOOD TO ALL THE
   BODY'S CELLS AND THE CELLS IN GRATITUDE OFFERING
   UP THEIR CARBON DIOXIDE....FINALLY TO BE EXHALED
   & BREATHED IN BY WAITING HUNGRY GREEN PLANTS
   THAT WE WILL FEAST ON IN PRAISE
   AND FEED OUR HUNGRY CELLS.....

WELL, YOU JUST WOULDN'T BELIEVE ALL THE WORK
   THAT GOES ON, AND THE AMAZING CO-LABORATION
   OF ALL THESE TINY BEINGS
   WHEN YOU ARE "BREATHED".

THIS IS GOING ON RIGHT NOW WHILE YOU ARE READING THIS,
   WITHOUT YOUR SLIGHT AWARENESS.
THERE IS THIS SEA OF GRACE RESIDING **INSIDE,**
   AS WELL AS **OUTSIDE** OF YOU.

AND IF YOU HAVE SEEN ANYONE'S **LAST BREATH,**
   YOU REALIZE WHAT A SACRED THING "BREATH" IS.
   IN THAT MOMENT ONE IS **NOT** "BREATHED INTO".
   THEY PASS FROM US. THEY GO ON.
   IT TAKES **_OUR_ BREATH** AWAY.
   TIME STOPS.....

AND I SAW MY DAUGHTER'S **FIRST BREATH,**
   AND THAT TOO, DISSOLVED ME AND THE PASSING OF TIME.
   I REMEMBER HOW SACRED THOSE BREATHS WERE.
   AND IF THEY ARE **ALL** SACRED,
   HOW THEN MIGHT WE LIVE?

EVERY BREATH CONNECTS US
   TO "THE BREATHER".

   IT IS OUR VISCERAL, TANGIBLE CONNECTION
      TO THE BELOVED, MOMENT BY MOMENT.

   IN THE MOST _MUNDANE_ ACT
      WE ARE BESTOWED WITH THE
      MOST _EXTRAORDINARY_ GIFT: "RUACH"
         BREATH...
            SPIRIT...
               WIND...

CEREMONY FOR LIFE-BREATH

Exhale fully.... Hold the emptiness ...
  until you are desperately hungry
  for the grace of breath......

Then, only then, receive a slow,
  huge in-breath from the Divine.
  FALL toward the BREATHER'S BREATH.
  Feel the Grace filling your being.
  It is pure energy re-creating you.
  Welcome back! You've been resuscitated!

THIS BREATH CONNECTS US TO THE **BREATHER...**

  AND TO ALL THE **HUMANS** ON THE PLANET
    WHO NOW RECEIVE A BREATH,

  AND TO ALL THE **ANIMALS**: FOUR-LEGGED, WINGED,
    CRAWLING ONES WHO RECEIVE A BREATH,

  AND TO ALL THE **PLANTS** WHO UNDER THEIR LEAVES OPEN
    THEIR "STOMAS: MOUTHS" TO RECEIVE A BREATH

WE'RE ALL BREATHING TOGETHER NOW.

  THE WHOLE EARTH RECEIVES
  A GREAT BREATH FROM THE **BREATHER,**
    AND IS ALIVE.
  THIS IS THE GREAT GIVE-AWAY
    PERMEATING THE WHOLE EARTH WITH GRACE

  AND, AS WE ALL BREATHE TOGETHER,
    WE ARE ONE
      WITH THE **ONE**.

2)SPIRIT-BREATH

"JESUS SAID,
'PEACE BE WITH YOU.
AS ABBA SENT ME,
SO I AM SENDING YOU.'
AFTER SAYING THIS
HE BREATHED (RUACH) ON THEM AND SAID:
'RECEIVE THE HOLY SPIRIT (RUACH).'"　　　JOHN 20:21

THIS IS THE 2ND GREAT BREATH.
THIS IS THE "DIVESTMENT".
JESUS **GIVES OVER** THE "**SPIRIT-BREATH**"
　　THAT ENERGIZED HIS JOURNEY—
　　THAT EMPOWERED HIS PRACTICES.

JESUS SAID THAT HIS FOLLOWERS
　　"WILL PERFORM THE **SAME WORKS** AS I DO MYSELF
　　AND WILL PERFORM EVEN **GREATER WORKS**..."
　　AFTER HE IS GONE.　　　　　JOHN 14:12

YOU HAD EVERYTHING YOU NEED
　　WITHOUT THIS —
　　IT WAS GIVEN IN THE 1ST BREATH, THE LIFE-BREATH.

NOW WITH THE SPIRIT-BREATH,
　　YOU HAVE
　　EVERYTHING
　　JESUS HAD!

DON'T MISS THIS!

IF YOU EVER FEEL WHINEY,
　　　　　WEAK, OR
　　　　　WOBBLY,
　　　　　CHECK THIS OUT.

THIS IS THE POWER
　　TO PARTNER
　　IN THE DIVINE BELOVED'S
　　OWN WORK.

WHAT MORE COULD ANYONE NEED...?
　　OR EVER WANT?

NOW LET'S SEE HOW THIS CAN BECOME **REAL**
　　FOR US.....

CEREMONY FOR SPIRIT-BREATH

WE WILL "ENTER" JOHN 20:21 AS PRINTED ABOVE:

YOU ARE STANDING BEFORE JESUS,
    HUNGRY FOR THE ENERGY THAT FILLS HIS BEING...
    LONGING FOR A TASTE OF THE FIRE INSIDE JESUS.....

JESUS SAYS, *"Peace be with you"*...

    AND YOU LET THAT ENVELOP YOU
    LIKE A MOTHER'S BLANKET COMFORTS HER CHILD.
    YOU FEEL SEEN...HELD... CONSOLED... CALMED...
    IT IS THE SHALOM OF GOD.

JESUS SAYS, *"As ABBA sent me, so I am sending you."*

    AND YOU REALIZE THAT THE WORK OF JESUS
        IS INCOMPLETE, AND SOMEHOW
        YOU ARE TO TAKE IT UP NOW.
    ALL YOUR LIFE HAS PREPARED YOU FOR THIS.
    ONLY YOU CAN DO WHAT YOU ARE TO DO.
    IT HAS TO DO WITH THE "REIGN OF SHALOM",
        AND, AS IN THE LORD'S PRAYER,
        IT NEEDS YOUR HANDS & HEART.

JESUS BREATHES INTO YOU SAYING,

        "Receive Ruach, the Spirit-Breath."

    THIS IS LIKE A RESUSCITATION OF YOUR
        SPIRIT- STARVED BODY.
    YOU REALIZE YOU HAVE BEEN JUST "**SURVIVING**".

    THIS IS A transfusion of fire
        INTO YOUR DARKENED BEING.

Breathe this in, again & again...
        AWAKEN THE WEARY CORNERS
        OF YOUR CONSCIOUSNESS.

THIS BREATH CONNECTS YOU INTIMATELY TO <u>JESUS</u>,
AND TO THE <u>WORK</u> OF GOD.
AS YOU BREATHE THIS IN,
HIS LIFE IS COMPLETING,
AND YOURS IS BEGINNING.

AND THIS Spirit-Breath,
THIS BREATH OF FIRE,
IS ABSOLUTELY, AND SURPRISINGLY

THE same Spirit,

THE same Fire,

THE same Power

THAT JESUS HAD.

NOW IT IS GIVEN TO YOU.
AND YOU ARE <u>**JOINED**</u> TO <u>**JESUS**</u>

AND TO <u>**ALL**</u> WHO HAVE INHALED
THE LIFE- BREATH,

AND TO <u>**ALL**</u> WHO HAVE DRAWN
THE SPIRIT-BREATH.

THERE IS A GREAT COMMUNITY
OVER THE CONTINENTS
AND OVER THE AGES.
YOU ARE A PART OF THAT.
IT IS THE COMMUNITY OF LIFE
& THE COMMUNION OF SAINTS.

WHEN YOU RECEIVE THE BREATH,
REMEMBER THIS.
<u>***YOU ARE NOT ALONE***</u>.

Breathe it in.
IT IS ALWAYS THERE FOR YOU.
IT IS A SPRING OF LIFE THAT DOESN'T RUN DRY.
IT IS THERE FOR YOU. BREATHE IT IN...

<u>**NOW TAKE UP THE PRACTICES OF JESUS**</u>.
THEY ARE UNIVERSAL, ARCHETYPAL, HUMAN.
ENTER THE SACRED WORK/ PLAY.

POSTLUDE

CAN YOU LIVE THE SPIRITUALITY OF JESUS TODAY?

YES, OR THIS HANDBOOK IS USELESS.
    BUT **NO**, IT WILL NOT BE EASY!

FOR EXAMPLE, LET'S TAKE THE ETHICS OF JESUS.......

"THE SAMARITANS WOULD NOT RECEIVE HIM
    BECAUSE HE WAS HEADING FOR JERUSALEM....
    (SAMARITANS WORSHIPED AT SAMARIA, NOT JERUSALEM)"
JAMES & JOHN SAID, "LORD, DO YOU WANT TO CALL DOWN
FIRE FROM HEAVEN TO BURN THEM UP (AS ELIJAH DID)?"
                                 LUKE 9:53F.

HERE WE HAVE JESUS' **OWN DISCIPLES UNABLE TO LIVE THE SPIRITUALITY OF JESUS.** WE COULD LOOK AT THEIR ETHICS IN THIS PERSPECTIVE:

ETHICS 101   UNLIMITED RETALIATION
    YOU HURT ONE OF US, WE TAKE OUT YOUR VILLAGE.
    GENESIS 19: *"THEN YHVH RAINED DOWN ON SODOM & GOMORRAH BRIMSTONE AND FIRE (VOLCANO?)...*
    ON ALL THE PEOPLE LIVING THERE".
    JESUS' DISCIPLES ABOVE ARE VENGEFUL
    AND SEE GOD IN THEIR **OWN** IMAGE.

ETHICS 201   LIMITED RETALIATION
    YOU HURT ONE OF US, WE HURT ONE OF YOU.
    EXODUS 21:24 *"IF HARM IS DONE...YOU WILL AWARD LIFE*
                         FOR LIFE, EYE FOR EYE..."
    THIS RESTRAINT IS **A GREAT ETHICAL ACHIEVEMENT**.

ETHICS 301   LIMITED LOVE.
    WE FORGIVE/RECONCILE IF YOU ARE **ONE OF US**.
    WE RETALIATE/AVENGE IF YOU ARE **NOT** ONE OF US.
    LEVITICUS 19:19: *"YOU WILL NOT EXACT VENGEANCE, OR HOLD A GRUDGE AGAINST THE MEMBERS OF YOUR RACE, BUT WILL LOVE YOUR NEIGHBOR AS YOURSELF."*

    MATTHEW 5:43: *"YOU HAVE HEARD IT SAID, 'YOU WILL LOVE YOUR NEIGHBOR AND HATE YOUR ENEMY..."*
    THIS WAS AN **ACHIEVEMENT IN HUMAN EVOLUTION**.

ETHICS 401 UNLIMITED LOVE
WE FORGIVE/RECONCILE WITH EVERYONE!
MATTHEW 5:44: *"I SAY TO YOU, LOVE YOUR ENEMIES,
PRAY FOR THOSE WHO PERSECUTE YOU...
GOD'S SUN RISES ON THE BAD & GOOD ALIKE."*

HERE WE SEEK TO ATTUNE TO GOD'S ETHIC.
GOD IS NOT IN OUR IMAGE,
    BUT WE ARE IN GOD'S IMAGE.
AN EGO SURRENDER ALLOWS GOD'S COMPASSION
    TO POUR INTO THE WORLD
    THROUGH YOU.
WE BECOME MYSTICAL CONDUITS OF DIVINE GRACE.

THE DISCIPLES FIND THEMSELVES IN ETHICS 101,
    UNLIMITED RETALIATION.
THEY HAVEN'T EVEN CAUGHT UP TO THE ETHICAL ACHIEVEMENTS
    OF THEIR OWN TRADITIONS.
THEY ARE CAUGHT IN **"TRIBAL RELIGION"**,
    ONLY NOW THE FOLLOWERS OF JESUS HAVE BECOME
    THE NEW "TRIBE".
YOU CAN ONLY IMAGINE HOW JESUS FELT.

IT'S VERY CLEAR TO ME THAT
    <u>WITHOUT</u> AN INFRASTRUCTURE OF GRACE,

    <u>WITHOUT</u> A DIRECT CONNECTION WITH
        THE DIVINE BELOVED,
    <u>WITHOUT</u> AN INNER LIFE THAT IS SUPPORTING US...

    WE **CANNOT LIVE** THE SPIRITUALITY OF JESUS.

    AND <u>WITHOUT</u> OTHER PEOPLE SUPPORTING US,
      IT WILL <u>BE DIFFICULT,</u>
      AND WE WILL <u>FALL BACK</u> INTO CHILDHOOD PATTERNS,

        INTO NARROW CULTURAL TRADITIONS,

        INTO AUTHORITARIAN RELIGION, INTO EMPTY CYNICISM,

        INTO A LONELY & DISCONNECTED EGO,

        INTO *FEAR*....

AND, I AM JUST AS CLEAR THAT

WITH THAT INFRASTRUCTURE...

WITH THAT DIVINE CONNECTION...

WITH THAT INNER LIFE... AND

WITH SOME SOUL-FRIEND OR COMMUNITY ALONGSIDE....

WE CAN LIVE THIS SPIRITUALITY OF JESUS,
AND **MOVE INTO THE NEW HUMAN,**
THE NEXT EVOLUTION OF OUR SPECIES.

THIS IS THE **MEANING OF JESUS' LIFE** ,

THIS IS **JESUS' PRAYER**.

THIS IS THE **DREAM OF JESUS**.

PEOPLE HAVE LOOKED AT JESUS' LIFE AND SAID:
"WOW, WHAT A *MAN*. HE'S NOT HUMAN!"

OTHERS SAID, "WHAT A *GOD*, LOOK WHAT GOD CAN DO!"

BUT SOME SAID,
**"LOOK AT WHAT GOD & A HUMAN BEING
CAN DO TOGETHER!"**

WE CAN DO THIS BECAUSE **GOD WANTS IT**,

AND THE **WORLD NEEDS IT**,

AND WE **LONG FOR IT**!

JESUS GIVES YOU

EVERYTHING

HE HAD....
HIS WISDOM
HIS PRACTICES

HIS SPIRIT:

"RUACH"

"BREATHE IT IN"

"INTO THE NIGHT OF JESUS"

JESUS SLEEPS,
   IMAGES SWIRL INSIDE...

AN ELDER PROPHET RISES TO SPEAK,
   NO WORDS COME OUT,
   BUT THE TREES CATCH FIRE,
   AND THE DEAD SIT UP TO LISTEN...

A CHILD ABANDONED DOES NOT
   CRY, BUT FALLS INTO INTIMATE
   EMBRACE OF THE HOLY ONE...

A COMPELLING WOMAN INVITES
   YOU TO HER.
   SHE HOLDS YOU WHOLLY
   AND YOU STOP SHAKING....

A LEPROUS MAN,
   PART OF HIS FACE MISSING,
   STRETCHES OUT HIS HAND,
   TOUCHES YOUR CHEST,
   AND YOUR GRIEF DISSOLVES...

AND THEN A CASCADE OF SCENES:
   A FRESH LOAF OF BREAD...
   LILIES SWAYING IN THE WIND...
   STARS IN THEIR FAMILIAR HOUSES...
   A TENDER KISS...
   THE BELONGING INSIDE A PRAYER...
   THE LUMINOUS PRESENCE GLOWING
   EVERYWHERE, EVERYWHERE...
   FILLING THE CHEST...

REPOSE...HEALING REST...SANCTUARY...
   YOU AWAKEN GENTLY
   AS IMAGES DEPART...

THE FRAGRANCE OF THE DAWN GARDEN
   COMES IN,
   AND YOU ARE STILL BEING HELD,
   SOMEHOW SAFE WITHIN,
   WHILE THE TERROR AND THE WONDER
   OF THE MORNING ARISE.

THE 6 PRACTICES OF JESUS' SPIRITUALITY

INWARD JOURNEY

1ST: *SACRED SPACE* – THE DAILY MEETING

2ND: *GRACE* – IMMERSION IN THE BELOVED

3RD: *FACE* – OWNING MY DARKNESS

OUTWARD JOURNEY

4TH: BE COMPASSIONATE

5TH: CREATE SPIRITUAL COMMUNITY

6TH: EMBRACING THE CALL

USING THE PRACTICES

HOW TO BEGIN:

YOU DON'T NEED TO READ THIS HANDBOOK!
YOU CAN BEGIN IN ANY OF THE SIX PRACTICES!
THIS IS NOT A LADDER YOU ASCEND!
    THE 5TH IS NOT "BETTER" OR MORE "ADVANCED"
        THAN THE 4TH.

THEY ARE ALL "DOORS" INTO THE
    SPIRITUALITY OF JESUS.

GO TO THE ONE YOU ARE LED TOWARD.
    OPEN IT, AND <u>GO IN</u>.
    SEE WHERE IT TAKES YOU.

THEN READ ABOUT THAT "DOOR".
    USE THIS AS A GUIDE.
    BUT DON'T LET YOUR READING OF THIS
    BECOME A <u>**SUBSTITUTE FOR PRACTICE.**</u>

    <u>THIS HANDBOOK WON'T CHANGE YOUR LIFE,</u>
    <u>BUT PRACTICING THE SPIRITUALITY OF JESUS WILL</u>.

IT'S A GREAT & TRANSFORMING JOURNEY.
    AND IT CAN <u>**START ANYWHERE**</u> ,
        EVEN WITH THE SMALLEST STEP.

SUGGESTIONS FOR A SPIRITUAL COMMUNITY

I TAUGHT THE SPIRITUALITY OF JESUS IN SMALL GROUPS
    FOR 25 YEARS.
I WROTE TWO BOOKS ON THIS SPIRITUALITY.
    THEY WERE EXTENSIVE AND A BIT OVERWHELMING.
I HAD JUST FINISHED THE SECOND ONE
    WHEN I STARTED A SERMON ON THE MORNING
    OF MY 65TH BIRTHDAY: MAY 6, 2007.
I HAD BEEN THE PASTOR OF THIS CHURCH FOR 34 YEARS,
    AND I KNEW I WAS GOING TO RETIRE SOON.
    AND THEN IT HIT ME THAT I NEEDED TO MAKE THIS
    PRACTICE OF JESUS' SPIRITUALITY SUCCINCT AND CLEAR
    AND ACCESSIBLE TO ANYONE.
    AND I KNEW THAT IT WAS TIME <u>**TO PRACTICE THIS**</u>
    <u>**AS A CONGREGATION**</u>, NOT A SMALL GROUP.

"USING THE PRACTICES" CONT. 140)

I WANTED TO LEAVE SOMETHING UNDERSTANDABLE,
USEFUL, AND YET FAITHFUL TO JESUS' SPIRITUALITY.

SO I BEGAN THIS PROJECT, AND FOR 2 YEARS
WE WORKED WITH THIS AS A CONGREGATION.
EVERY SUNDAY WE PRINTED THE 6 PRACTICES
IN THE BULLETIN AS ABOVE,
AND EVERY SERMON RELATED TO IT IN SOME WAY.
WE TALKED ABOUT IT AT MEETINGS
AND RELATED IT
TO THE ISSUES THAT CAME UP.
VISITORS TO CHURCH GOT A SENSE OF
WHAT WE WERE ABOUT EASILY.
AND THEY WERE INVITED INTO OUR "EXPERIMENT".
IT BEGAN TO SHAPE US, IDENTIFY US.

IT GAVE US A LANGUAGE TO TALK
ABOUT OUR OWN JOURNEY.
IT WAS UP-FRONT, AND IN THE OPEN.
WHEN YOU HAVE A SMALL GROUP DOING THIS IN A
CONGREGATION, OTHERS CAN FEEL LEFT OUT.
BUT NOW NO ONE WAS LEFT OUT.
IT WAS SIMPLE ENOUGH TO MEMORIZE,
YET CHALLENGED US DOWN INTO OUR VISCERA.
THIS IS ONE WAY TO USE THIS.

SUGGESTIONS FOR A SMALL GROUP

GATHER A GROUP THAT WOULD LIKE
TO EXPLORE THIS TOGETHER.
MEET AT LEAST ONCE A MONTH,
TWICE IS BETTER, WEEKLY IS BEST.
MORE THAN 12 PEOPLE IS HARD,
EVEN 2 OR 3 PEOPLE CAN WORK.
SHARE A MEAL TOGETHER, IF YOU LIKE,
AND GET THE AMBIANCE OF THE "TABLE OF JESUS".
ESTABLISH CONFIDENTIALITY.
THIS WILL GET PERSONAL, HOPEFULLY.
LET EACH PERSON SHARE THEIR EXPERIENCE
OF THEIR LIVING RIGHT NOW.
"WHAT IS IT LIKE TO BE YOU"...
OR ASK: "HOW IS YOUR SOUL".
THEN DISCUSS THE TOPICS IN THIS HANDBOOK,
OR HOW ONE OF THE PRACTICES IS CHALLENGING YOU
RIGHT NOW.

AS YOU CONTINUE TO MEET BE SURE TO **GIVE EACH**
      A CHANCE TO TALK ABOUT THEIR EXPERIENCE OF A
      PARTICULAR PRACTICE THEY HAVE BEGUN.
      THE DANGER, OF COURSE, IS LETTING ONE OR TWO
      MORE VOCAL PEOPLE DOMINATE THE GROUP.
      GOING AROUND THE GROUP HELPS QUIETER PEOPLE.
      AND IF YOU NEED TO, YOU CAN HAVE A TIME LIMIT TO
      BALANCE THE CONVERSATIONS

SUPPORT THOSE WHO STRUGGLE, AND **WE ALL DO**.
      ENCOURAGE EVERYONE TO STRETCH THEMSELVES
      INTO NEW TERRITORY.
      IMAGINE JESUS CHALLENGING PEOPLE TO ENTER
      PLACES THAT HE HAS HIMSELF GONE, AND LET THAT
      "FIERCE TENDERNESS" AND "HEART-LONGING"
      BE AMONG YOU.

SUGGESTIONS FOR A PERSON

STUDY THE HANDBOOK
      AND JOURNAL YOUR EXPERIENCES AS IF
      YOU WERE REPORTING TO SOMEONE ELSE.
BE CREATIVE! FIND YOUR OWN APPROACH TO THIS AND
      ADAPT IT TO YOUR SITUATION.
THIS WILL TAKE A LOT OF DISCIPLINE,
      BUT IT CAN BE DONE.
HOWEVER, I WOULD ALSO BE ON THE LOOK-OUT
      FOR SOMEONE WHO MIGHT BE A GUIDE, PARTNER,
      COMPANION, COACH, FRIEND...
      THERE IS SOMEONE OUT THERE
      WHO WOULD LOVE THE INVITATION.

NEED HELP?

IF I CAN BE OF HELP, CONTACT ME FOR SUGGESTIONS.
OR , I COULD DO A WORKSHOP TO INTRODUCE THIS WHOLE PROJECT TO
YOUR CONGREGATION OR COMMUNITY. I HAVE LED GROUPS IN
"EXPERIENCING" THE SPIRITUALITY OF JESUS BY ENACTING ONE OF THE
TRANSFORMING EXPERIENCES OF JESUS' SPIRITUAL JOURNEY.
THIS IS A GREAT WAY OF LAUNCHING A GROUP OR CONGREGATION INTO
THIS ADVENTURE TOGETHER.

I CAN BE REACHED BY **PHONE AT 815-398-1634**
      OR **E-MAIL AT JAROB401@AOL.COM**

[1] **GOING HOME: JESUS AND BUDDHA AS BROTHERS**
THICH NHAT HANH (RIVERHEAD BOOKS, N.Y., 1999)
LIVING BUDDHA, LIVING CHRIST
THICH NHAT HANH (RIVERHEAD BOOKS, N.Y., 1995)

[2] **BREAKTHROUGH** (MEISTER ECKHART'S SERMONS)
MATTHEW FOX (IMAGE BOOKS, N.Y., 1980)
MEDITATIONS WITH MEISTER ECKHART
MATTHEW FOX (BEAR & CO., SANTA FE , 1983)

[3] **SYNOPSIS QUATTUOR EVANGELIORUM**
KURT ALAND (WURTTEMBERGISCHE BIBELANSTALT STUTTGART, GERMANY, 1964)

[4] **WHAT DO YOU ADVISE?** FRITZ KUNKLE
(IVES WASHBURN, N.Y., 1946)

[5] **PRAYERS OF THE COSMOS** NEIL DOUGLAS-KLOTZ
(HARPER & ROW, N.Y., 1990)
THE HIDDEN GOSPEL NEIL DOUGLAS-KLOTZ
(QUEST BOOKS, WHEATON,ILL., 1999)
THE HOLY BIBLE FROM ANCIENT EASTERN MANUSCRIPTS
GEORGE LAMSA (HOLMAN, PHILADELPHIA, 1933)

[6] **ILLUMINATIONS OF HILDEGARD OF BINGEN** MATTHEW FOX
(BEAR & CO., SANTA FE, 1985)

[7] **SELECTED POEMS OF RAINER MARIA RILKE** TRANS. ROBERT BLY
(HARPER & ROW, N.Y., 1981)

[8] **THE KABIR BOOK** VERSIONS BY ROBERT BLY
(BEACON PRESS, BOSTON, 1977)

[9] **ONE RIVER, MANY WELLS** MATTHEW FOX
(TARCHER/PUTNAM, N.Y., 2000)

[10] **GITANJALI** RABINDRANATH TAGORE
(SCRIBNER, N.Y., 1997)

[11] **LOVE POEMS FROM GOD** DANIEL LADINSKY
(PENGUIN COMPASS, N.Y., 2002)

[12] **LET YOUR LIFE SPEAK** PARKER PALMER
(JOSSEY-BASS, SAN FRANCISCO, 2000)

[13] **THE ESSENTIAL RUMI** TRANS. COLEMAN BARKS/J.MOYNE
(HARPERCOLLINS, N.Y., 1995)

[14] POEM BY HAFIZ, SOURCE UNKNOWN. FOR HAFIZ POETRY, SEE
THE GIFT TRANS. DANIEL LADINSKY
(PENGUIN PUTNAM N.Y., 1999)

QUOTES FROM THE BIBLE ARE FROM:

NEW REVISED STANDARD VERSION BIBLE
(NATIONAL COUNCIL OF CHURCHES/ NELSON, NASHVILLE, 1989)
NEW JERUSALEM BIBLE
(DOUBLEDAY, N.Y., 1985)
AUTHORIZED/ KING JAMES VERSION (1611)

About the Author

James A. Roberts is an ordained pastor in the Lutheran Church having served as chaplain at Elgin State Hospital (Illinois), and churches in Wilkes-Barre, Penn., and Rockford, Illinois.

He is co-founder of Manitoumie Retreat Center in Wisconsin, Four Winds Center for Spiritual Ecology, and Green Communities Coalition in Rockford, Illinois.

Author of *"The 3rd Species"*, a manifesto on the healing of the Creation.

He is a musician & poet and leads retreats, ceremonies, and inter-spiritual events.

He has three grown children and lives in Rockford, Illinois with his wife, Sallyann , and two salukis.